A Message From the Author:

I'm not a psychologist, social worker, guru, nor mad genius (that last one's debatable.) I'm just a guy who has lived many lives, and learned how to enjoy them. This book was written for the purpose of entertainment with an enlightening undertone. What you take from it is entirely up to you. This is how I've survived the turbulence I've encountered throughout my flight, and the advice given is tongue in cheek, with some true heart sprinkled on top. If you love to love, and laugh, then you'll enjoy this read. The experiences you'll discover inside are my own, so don't you go judgin' me, now. Live your own life, and I'll offer you the same courtesy. I just want you to enjoy the days you have left on this rock, and wake up with a story now and then. If you don't have at least a few good ones, then what was the point? Here's how I did it, and will continue to do so, until I slide sideways and barrel roll into a casket.

What are people saying about
How to Survive When the Bottom Drops Out?

His philosophy to move on pervades this little book and his story could be something of an inspiration to many who find themselves in similar straits.
Harold S Writer, reviewer for the *Ontonagon Herald*

Honest, heartfelt and hilarious, it is well worth a read and re-read.
Sean Taylor

Read this book and be humbled for many of us will never meet someone like this...
Tony Johnson

If that is what you are used to from a self help book then be warned, and be prepared to laugh your ass off.
Cisthebigdog

We don't all reach the highs or descend to the depths that J.T. has managed but life will pull the rug from under most of us sometime. Here is how to pick the rug back up and beat life about the head with it.
Carolyn Steele

He bares his soul so that we can see our own and leads us to believe that an imperfect life is perfection personified.
Kim B

How to Survive
When the Bottom Drops Out

A semi-autobiographical/somewhat comical "How To" guide by a guy who's been there... and shit the bed...more than twice.

forged by
J. T. Sather

Published by
Inknbeans Press

Cover: Paul S. Beegle (photo)
Custom Cover Creations (design)

© 2012 J.T. Sather
© 2013 J.T. Sather and Inknbeans Press

ISBN-13: 978-0615771786 (Inknbeans Press)
ISBN-10: 0615771785

Author's Note

The names have not been changed to protect the innocent. There aren't any.

About the Author

I grew up your typical Midwest boy. Graduated high school in '86, I did what all the cool kids were doing: got a factory job, married my girlfriend Bekka Sue, had a baby named Amber Nicole, and moved up the ladder in my crappy, brainless factory position.

I was living the American dream, baby! I had two cars in the driveway, a three bedroom house, a newborn little girl, my fair share of motorcycles and your standard man-type toys, and a beautiful wife to boot. Life was grand.

Then one year later the factory my wife and I both worked in closed down. Oh, shit! Now what? My only skill at that point was running the machine that made reel-to-reel computer tape!

Big demand for that, right? Maybe ten years prior but now I was f'd in the a**! Did I mention that I was at the ripe old age of 19?! Something had to be done and fast.

I tried my own janitorial business with my friend Dave for a minute and worked several other occupational hazards to no avail. There just wasn't enough money to be made from what I was doing. The Midwest was pretty tight in those days. The decision had to be made: "Go West young moron!"

So off to Las Vegas we went and I jumped head first into the construction biz. Now, mind you, I didn't have the faintest idea of what I was doing. My only skill was cutting the tape on the take-up machine at five thousand feet and put it in the storeroom to cure for forty eight hours, whatever that means.

Well, naturally, my beautiful young bride couldn't be patient with me while I beat my head against the wall learning how to do something entirely foreign to me, so she left.

It was probably three months later that I started business number two, but this time I tripled my income overnight! Unfortunately, I was a bit despondent over my divorce, so I threw myself into my work. That's the good part; I learned tons about how to build everything under the sun and how to make loads of money doing it. It would have been handy if I had learned how to save it. In the course of the next ten years, I partied my ass off and managed to piss away a cool million. Oops.

Then I met number two, Julie Ann. I had been a playboy for a decade and by this time my business was really peaking. I was in my early thirties, and I was sure she was the one, so I married her. We lived the good life for eight years.

Then came the dreaded year of 2009.

All of my grand delusions of retiring by forty-five were completely crushed like a juicy overripe grape under the stinky foot of recession. The universe, as I knew it, had shit down my neck.

What's interesting is that it only took me seven years to piss away the next million, so at least I was getting good at it! I would tell my wife, "Spend all you want, I'll make more!"

"How much did you save?" you ask. I think I'll plead the fifth on that one.

In the course of this spectacular year, my awesome Rottweiler of eight years was hit by a truck and killed. Doesn't every sad song start with "My dog died"? My business tanked as most construction companies did. My work truck was repossessed I lost my three boats, travel trailer, dirt bikes and other man-type toys, including beautiful wife number two, who took my new Rottweiler pup, Otto, with her. My future son in law and father of my grandson hung himself. About halfway through the year I lost my house.

This final straw, or so I thought, sent me into a tailspin of epic proportions. I spend three strange days in a drunken, self-pity stupor. At eight AM on day three, I ended up in a horrific head on collision, totaling that truck and nearly totaling myself. I can only thank the powers that be that the poor guy that hit me (who was actually wearing his seatbelt, unlike my dumb ass) was uninjured, because I spent most of September in a coma. I nearly died on the table...twice. I suffered mild brain damage, shattered my eye socket, jacked up my right shoulder and got a shiny new titanium plate installed in my head.

When I was finally released from the hospital I was forced to come to the realization that my business, marriage, and general way of life were over...again. I had become a walking, talking country song. At least the doctors were able to restore my smashing good looks!

After I was released from the hospital, I decided it was time to make a retreat to the Midwest for some rest and recuperation. I was gone less than two months when the phone call came in. It was my good friend Tom calling to inform me that the only thing of value I had left (that I was storing in his backyard) had been stolen: My 1998 Harley Davidson FLH 1340cc police bike. Did I mention my dog's name was Harley? Stephen King could not have written a more horrifying script for me, and yet there it was. Irony is a fickle thing.

Upon hearing this news, I immediately burst into hysterical laughter. It was at this pivotal moment that I finally got the joke. That's when it hit me that I'd been using the wrong scorecard the whole time.

[joke: the ridiculous element in something]

The year I had would have killed the average man. Good thing I'm not the average man. It was time to step out of the painting and analyze the brush strokes.

Prelude

This guide is for those of you who find yourselves basking in a vat of your own feces, or trying to avoid it. It can happen to the best of us. Not everyone is predestined to crash and burn, yet it doesn't mean you can travel without uninsured motorist coverage.

I've been on both sides of the fence more than twice. This gives me a shinier crystal ball than the average bear.

There is a right way and a wrong way to plod through this conscious daydream called life we all share. Have you ever done one of those silly tests for a job, guidance counselor, or your parole officer where they offer you a ridiculous hypothetical question, and then right before you answer they interject with "Now there is no right or wrong answer?" Bullshit. You can bet your ass there is. Of course, no one is going to tell you this because they are trying to determine if you have already solved the riddle on your own. Most haven't.

Everyone gets a second chance. Hell, some get a seventeenth chance! Sadder yet, some waste the opportunities they've been handed on a silver platter. It boils down to what you make of 'the chance or chances you get'. More importantly what are you willing to put into it? You don't get the good stuff in life by sitting on your ass and hoping it will just happen on its own.

I have had a good life so far, and I don't complain repeatedly about the crappy turn the game has made. I understand that with each pass of the dice, it's that much closer to my go and the amusement will continue.

Each roll of the dice offers a limited combination of possibilities, so the trick is to make sure the board you're playing on is a fun one. If every other square is

"Do not pass go, do not collect two hundred dollars, go directly to jail" then you're playing the wrong game.

There is no such thing as "The man is keeping me down". There are plenty of things that can knock you down. The only thing that can keep you there is you. It's time to buckle up and drive.

I'm going to give you some simple tricks of the trade that most people are unaware of. All you need is a basic set of hand tools and a good attitude. All of the heavy equipment to get the job done will be provided for you, if you're up to the task.

Open a beer, listen up and enjoy the orientation! Use caution, and don't cut yourself turning the pages.

[orientation: the act or process of being intellectually, emotionally, or functionally directed]

Chapter 1:
The Point

So you think you deserve to live, eh. Why? I'm not judging you. I don't even know you! I just think it's a question you should ask yourself every now and then. Sometimes you have to ask yourself what you think of you. Your answer might surprise you.

If you cannot come up with a good answer, then please refer to Chapter 18 now.

If your answer is "I need to live for my kids," then you already have one foot in the grave. Refer to Chapter 18 immediately.

Now that we have established there is a reason to be here, we can administer some first aid.

[first aid: emergency care]

What I'm about to share with you is designed to give you some insight on how to get your shit together so you can rebuild your empire. The following should help you focus enough to begin the ascent back to the place you were, and beyond.

With a steady approach and a little luck, you just might stay there this time.

Chapter 2:
The Assessment

[assessment: to make an official valuation of property]

Stop! Don't move a muscle! Trust no one! And for God's sake, don't panic!! OK, you can trust me, 'cause I don't know where you live, but put a lock on everything you have (if there is anything) and listen sharp.

This is potentially the most critical phase you're going to face. If, for some reason, you feel you can skip this phase, then you've just added three years to your recovery and subtracted seven years from your life expectancy.

Remember the old adage "you can't take it with you?" Well, the same theory applies when you fall into the abyss. The sooner you believe me, the faster you can move forward. Keep in mind its just stuff. You can always get more stuff. Now is the time to make the stuff you have left (while you still have some) work for you. If you waste precious time worrying about the crap you've compiled over the years, you'll just end up losing it anyway, get nothing for it, and develop a bleeding ulcer for your trouble. You need to face the facts, it's time to liquidate.

Step 1

You must have a proper inventory of what you have left. Write it down in two separate lists. This will give you a better understanding of what you have to work with.

[The first list: stuff that might be worth something.]

This is an important one. If the bottom has dropped out, you're going to need every dollar you can get. Beer doesn't grow on trees, you know! Once you have completed the list, I want you to put a price next to each item. Not what you paid for it, but what you think its actual worth.

Now have a garage sale and get rid of it...all of it. Oh, and those silly price tags you came up with? Yeah, throw that pipe dream out the window. Be prepared to accept any offer for any of it.

Through the course of the sale, one of two things must become evident. Either a large sum of money will begin to materialize in front of you, giving you the grubstake you need to start over, or you'll find that most people won't give you lead for what you thought was worth gold— probably the latter.

The good news is it's a win-win either way. If the first comes true, the benefit speaks for itself. If the second is true, then you can purge a lot of junk from your cache.

[purge: to free from moral or ceremonial defilement; to make free of something unwanted]

The difficult realization of the second scenario is that, at some point, you're going to have to re-evaluate the manner in which you decide what's worth holding on to, and what's just junk.

Understand that I'm not saying you should never own anything -- quite the contrary. I've had it all more than once and will certainly have the things I want again. What I am saying is to recognize when it's time to liquidate. Remember, one man's junk is just going to end up another man's junk. The only difference is whether or not you get anything for it before it's too late. Will you please let it go so we can move forward? Thank you.

[The second list: the keepers]

This list consists of all the memorabilia you've collected about your life. About your life, not a football signed by Brett Favre (wait, that's pretty cool). I think you get my point.

Condense these items into a two foot cube. It's time to travel light my friend. If it doesn't fit in the box, then throw the rest of that crap away. You can't move forward if you won't let go of the past.

Make sure it's a sturdy vessel. It has to be something that can survive the test of time. I've got the last thirty years of my life condensed into a 1978 forest green metal Coleman cooler. I've been dragging this thing around the country for a long, long time. It's one of those things I would stuff in the rafters of the garage for ten years at a time until I needed to vacate said premises.

It's like an escape pod for your shit. Not the couch or the VCR but the irreplaceable shit. You can buy a new TV. You can't buy the scraps of paper you've collected over the decades that define you as a unique member of society. Not unless you're Picasso or Andy Warhol, but then you're not or you wouldn't need to read this book.

When the shit hits the fan, it's awfully handy to be able to grab your stuff quick. No matter where I've ended up through the years, I have always had my "hope chest." It's fun to look inside. It's like a tiny time capsule of my bizarre life. I've got love letters from Bekka Sue that she wrote to me when she was still in high school. The track spikes my best friend Paul wore in 1985 when he won the 300 meter low hurdles in the state finals (I've always said I was going to have them bronzed. I'll get to it...eventually.) There's also a Xerox copy of Amber's hands when she was less than two years old. Ya know, the important stuff.. You only get to keep this stuff if it fits in the box. It's worth paying the thirty-five dollar extra baggage fee to throw it on the plane with you. It is not worth having to rent a U-haul for four hundred dollars and spending a grand on gas to haul a bunch of shit across the country just so you can throw it away someplace else.

When the shit hit the fan the last time, I stuffed my three bedroom house into a ten foot by twenty foot storage unit. This was after Julie had proclaimed that she had already taken what she wanted from the house. One year later I finally moved into another house. When I went to my storage unit to retrieve my precious goods, I discovered that my lovely ex-bride (who had just moved into her own apartment two weeks prior), had cleaned me out. The only things left were my stereo, pool table, my clothes and three boxes of crappy books that I didn't want to read the first decade they rotted on our bookshelf! The only books I wanted were the Louis L'Amour collector's edition hard copies but naturally those were not to be found. I'm sure she didn't even know who Louis L'Amour was. I'll bet her new boyfriend did. That storage fee was well spent. When I told you to put a lock on your stuff, I forgot to tell you to make damn sure nobody else has a key! Don't even let anyone know where your shit is!

I spent the next two years in my new digs. It was truly an awesome pad. It had four bedrooms, a giant great room with a fireplace and cathedral ceiling, a sauna in the master bath, and an indoor pool. How could I afford this you ask? Free rent (I'll explain how that's done in Chapter 3). Getting back to the point, after two years the bank finally evicted me. It's amazing how much crap you can acquire in two years, even when you're not working (I'll explain how that's done in Chapter 4.)

This time I condensed my newfound treasure onto my fourteen foot flatbed motorcycle trailer, minus the motorcycles of course, and stored this pile in my daughter, Deborah's garage. After one year in her garage (and in her way...I love you honey!), I finally decided it was time to liquidate and split town.

Here comes the tragic realization.

I had a garage sale and much to my dismay I discovered I had a lot more lead than gold. I made a total of $700, including the sale of the trailer itself. The best part, Xander (19 years old) had to handle it because I went to jail on a frickin' eleven year old traffic warrant I didn't even know I had.

He spent the money keeping his own ass out of jail. Ironic, isn't it? Although I was happy my boy was able to pay his fines and avoid incarceration, I was still a bit miffed.

[miffed: put into an ill humor; offended]

That was going to be my "get out of Dodge" money. Now I was trapped for a minute. In light of these events, I will never store anything ever again...ever. If you don't have a place for it, you don't need it. Get rid of it.

Step 2

The next stage of your assessment is the vehicle. Do you still have one? Does it need a shitload of work— or more importantly— do you still have a driver's license? I'll tell you straight up, if you do not have a driver's license then you need to sell your car, truck, whatever. Don't worry about how you're going to get to work, assuming you have any. Catch a ride with a friend, take the bus, or walk.

You cannot rebuild yourself with the constant threat of jail time looming over your head. I hold this truth to be self-evident, as I am writing this chapter from my cell and I don't mean phone. Lesson learned. Next.

Assuming your vehicle is in good shape and you can still operate it legally, then, by all means, keep it. Reliable transportation is something too many Americans take entirely for granted. But if not, then it's time to get rid of it. We're going to rebuild you from the ground up, and there is no room for junk. Purge, purge, purge.

Chapter 3:
Where Are You Going to Live?

This can be a tricky one. You need to reside somewhere. Under an overpass is not the best option... (long, drawn out pause)...yet.

There's always another alternative. You just have to swallow your pride and talk to friends and/or family and explain your situation. The people in your life are there for you more than you think. Transversely, you will definitely have the opportunity to identify and eliminate the ones that are not. Fair weather friends are not worth having. They're fun to have a drink with or tell a joke but beyond that, they have no further use. Sooner or later it's going to rain, and when it does, it's nice to know who's holding an umbrella.

If you find that you have no place to turn, then you should refer to Chapter 19.

So, there I was, minding my own business, twenty thousand feet, naked without a parachute.

[**parachute: a device for slowing the descent of a person.** Can it be any more literal than that> What a handy apparatus.]

All of the sudden, from out of nowhere, Mike, my landlord of the past eight years evicted me for being two weeks late on my rent. I didn't even have an airbag to land on. What a prick! I didn't see that one coming. At that point I was still working, be it ever so slightly.

Instead of panicking, I buckled up. "OK," I said to myself, "time to get a grip."

Now the wife had already been gone for a few months but my twenty year old daughter, Deborah, her one year old son, Jaden (my grandson), and my sixteen year old boy, Xander, stayed with me.

Looking back at it, I realize now that if I would have worried more about myself instead of everyone else, I probably would not have been evicted and we would've still had a place to live.

It's become my golden rule. You see, by concentrating on yourself, there is a byproduct. You will simply have the things to offer others in need without such apprehension. My biggest fear was "What's going to happen to my kids?" I worried so much about it that I forgot to worry about myself! Shit, if I would have worried more about me in the first place, I'd probably still be married. It turns out nobody wants to live with a sad sack.

Well, that's all hindsight by this point. Now it's time for you to figure out what to do with yourself. The first thing you need to do is rely on your friends. That's why you have them and that's why they have you. It's a two-way street we're all careening on.

[**careen: to sway from side to side being pulled wildly by a team of runaway horses**. That pretty much sums up my life!]

Back in the long, long time ago, when Bekka Sue and I split up, my best pal Paul was in Corpus Christi, Texas going through the same thing with his first wife. He was a Coastie at the time and his term was almost up.

After talking on the phone for a while, we both understood that neither of us was in good shape. Paul said to me, "either you're coming to Texas, or I'm coming to Vegas. What's it going to be?"

I was running a department at M & M Electric at the time, so I said, "you come here and I'll have a job for you when you hit the ground." He was on a plane in less than a week.

We both buried ourselves into our jobs by day and then we would party our guts out by night. I like to think neither one of us would have survived the ordeal if we didn't cover each other's backsides.

We had some outrageous times. I think I'll save most of our exploits for the "how to get some action under any circumstances" guide. I think I could write volumes on that one, but there is one classic tale I must share with you.

We were renting rooms from our friend Mark, who had just split up with his wife. It's funny how birds of a feather flop together. We had been there about a week when we thought it was time for some house warming debauchery.

[**debauchery: extreme indulgence**, a.k.a., in fun and games]

There must have been fifty people or more by seven o'clock. I concocted a batch of jungle juice in a couple of watermelon halves and we partied like rock stars.

Paul found himself a pretty young thing and, at some point, they disappeared. She was a cute girl, although a little plump. After a few hours, I thought I should knock on his door and check to see if he was still alive. When I tapped on the door he said, "Come in."

I entered the room and he was alone, lying on his bed. I said, "What happened to what's-her-face?" (Oh my goodness, I think her name was Laura! Funny how some things you don't forget. Maybe it was because my first wife ran off with her husband.) He informed me, "I sent her out the window." He didn't want anyone to know he was with a chubby chick. Man, I laughed my ass off. Picturing her bumbling out the window was priceless!

Those were some damn fun times. He only stayed for less than a year, but I will remember those times forever. I was honored to offer him my couch. Good thing, too, because I ended up on his couch after my car accident nineteen years later. Karma strikes again!

If couch surfing were an Olympic sport, I would take home the gold every time. I've done a lot of it through the decades, and it's kept me alive. There are simple rules you need to apply to keep your friends. Do not take advantage, become a burden, or get in the way. Simply be yourself and treat the time spent as an extended vacation with someone's company that you both enjoy.

The key word here is both.

If you're having a good time staying with a friend and he/she gets sick of your dumb ass, then you didn't play by the rules.

Try not to stay in any one place for too long. The last thing you want to do is wear out your welcome and be that three-day old, stinky fish in the fridge. Help out around the place and make yourself useful. Be a good guest and, when you move on, leave them wanting more, not relieved to get rid of you.

Right now I'll assume you are not working. Worst-case scenario is always the best approach (this is why it's imperative to follow Chapter 2.) You're going to need some money. Search for it. There is always some kind of work that needs to be done somewhere. The hard part is biting the bullet and taking a cut in pay. Less money than you're used to sucks, but not as badly as having no money at all.

In the construction business, as I was back then, 2009 was a nightmare. Sunny Las Vegas was no longer the big boom town it used to be. When I first got here in

'89, I fell into the swimming pool business. It was a great way to get my feet wet! At that time more than a hundred pool contractors were in the valley. By 2009, I think there were ten.

If there was a pool to be built, it was like dropping a single goldfish in a barrel full of piranha. It gave a whole new meaning to "dog eat dog." There just weren't enough scraps left out there for this pup. You need to adapt.

I found myself pressure washing driveways, installing Pergo flooring, painting (and I hate painting), whatever I could get my hands on. I've always said, "I can build you an airplane, but you're painting it yourself." Nowadays, you have to be willing to do whatever it takes to put some green in your pocket.

After I was evicted, I stayed with friends for about six months. I went to Illinois, upper Michigan, down to Illinois again and wound up back in Vegas. When I got back, I stayed with my daughter Deborah for a little while. She was doing all right and had a nice place of her own. It was wonderful spending time with her family.

One fine spring day my good friend Joe called to tell me he was moving to San Francisco. He asked if I would stay in his house in Vegas and watch his Great Dane, Maximus. I had loved the beast since he was a pup. It seemed like a great idea, so I took him up on it.

Joe was in the process of trying to get a loan modification and, therefore, wasn't paying his mortgage. He told me he didn't feel right charging me rent, so the only bills I had were utilities and dog food.

This is probably the best thing you can hope for.. A cool pad with no rent— there's more of them out there than you think. It's not a permanent solution, but it can certainly get you past a hump.

I realize the place sounded great on paper, but it was in the midst of remodel. There was no kitchen, no AC, and no furnace. This is where improvisation is your friend. I had a microwave, a rice cooker, a hotplate, toaster oven, George Foreman grill, and a Coleman camping BBQ outside. Given these fine apparatuses, I could cook a Thanksgiving feast fit for a king and I did.

I had a swamp cooler in the window for summer and in the fireplace I burnt anything flammable to get through the winter. Cozy! It seems empty beer boxes are a fabulous fire starter.

I enjoyed the piss out of it. That house was, by far, my favorite campsite. We all affectionately called it "the cave." All I had to do was mention in passing that I had an indoor pool and, in less than an hour, I had a naked nymph in the water. It was AWESOME!

I stayed in this house for two years, somehow managing to survive. I had lots of really good friends who would stop by with a case of beer. Beer is essential to survival...and heat. We would play dominos and contemplate the universe. It was a good time.

About a year into it, I found myself having a hard time paying the power bill. My water had been off for about four days. That didn't bother me too badly. I took baths in the pool. All you need is a five gallon bucket and you can use the pool to flush the toilet. However, there is no substitute for power, at least not a legal one.

My friend Tom was a little down on his luck at the same time. He was living with his ex-family-in-law only a block away from me. He called me up and said, "Hey, I'm feeling a little stifled here. Can I stay with you a couple days, maybe, I don't know."

I thought for about a half a second and replied, "help me pay the utilities and it's no problem." Two days later, he and his girlfriend moved in. Well, that problem was solved. Enter another chapter of fun and games.

Tom considered himself a superior dominologist, as did I. We played many a drunken game of bones into the wee hours of the night. He was also a construction guy feeling the crunch of the '09 landslide. We had a lot in common.

His girl, Stacey, and I would sit up all hours of the night, contemplating why the world turns around and such like. We helped each other solve many personal issues. It's always good to have someone to talk to when things are not their best. It can relieve loads of stress and anxiety.

Much like anything, all good things must pass. The bank finally stopped working with Joe and we eventually got the boot. It was time to liquidate again and dust off my couch surfing board. I still wasn't working much to speak of, but I found a small job here and there. It was enough to supply beer money, but not much else. It was still my plan to leave town for a while, but I needed a decent project to finance it.

P. S., never leave home without a parachute. You never know when you're going to be thrown off the plane.

Chapter 4:
How to Acquire Stuff When You're Not Working

[stuff: a group or scattering of miscellaneous objects]

Now that you have a place, you're gonna have to acquire a new batch of stuff. When you're riding the couch wave you tend to take the things people have in their houses for granted, the little things that you simply expect to be there. You know, like a spoon, coffee table, coffee cup, or...coffee. When you move into a house of your own and you have only the clothes on your back, it can prove to be a tad inconvenient.

Assuming that you're not working, there are ways to gather such items without spending money. It takes a little resourcefulness but it can be done. The key word here is "resourcefulness", not "scam artist."

Keep your ear to the ground for any of your friends who are leaving town. This will be the best opportunity for you to gather essential goods and whatnot.

When I moved into "the cave," Joe, who had moved to California, left me a bed, a dining table, and two chairs in the house. That was the extent of my furnishing. After a few weeks, I found myself sitting at the table in the middle of a giant great room staring at my laptop. Upon looking around the room, I noticed the place looked a might sparse.

[sparse: less plentiful than what is normal, necessary, or desirable]

It was like sitting at a card table in the middle of a high school gymnasium— by yourself. It was just a wee bit agoraphobic. I received a phone call from my friend,

15

Justben, who asked me if I wanted a couch. "Well, sure," I said. When he showed up, it turned out to be the biggest couch I had ever seen. A giant sectional with two reclining chairs and a queen size fold out bed! It was the perfect thing for that big ass living room. It turned out he and his wife, April, were moving to Belgium.

Justben went first (it's not Benjamin, it's just Ben) to start a new job, leaving April in charge of packing up the house and putting everything in storage. When she asked me for help, I was more than happy to oblige.

With each room we cleared out, she asked me, "Do you need this? Do you want that?" By the time we were done I had a couple of cool chairs, more kitchen stuff than I knew what to do with, a bunch of towels, and a cool pub clock that I hung over the fireplace. Oh yeah, and a kegerator!

This happened two more times in the three months that followed! I had fewer friends living in town, but I had more stuff than I had lost in my storage unit!

Suddenly, I had a comfortable place again. It's strange how things work out. I simply followed my golden rule and everything worked out. These were friends that I would have helped do anything in the first place. Helping them made me feel good and the byproduct was that I ended up with the things they didn't need anymore but I needed badly.

When you acquire goodies in this fashion and it comes time to liquidate again, keep in mind how you got this stuff. If you have someone you know in need of stuff, donate what you can. Keeping your Karma rolling is going to be a major factor when you rebuild the next time.

[**Karma: the force generated by a person's actions held to perpetuate transmigration and in its**

ethical consequences to determine the nature of the person's next existence. Holy shit, don't piss her off!]

Karma is like a really hot ex-girlfriend. She can be happy to see you again and give you a big sloppy kiss or she can go psycho, jump on your back and scratch your eyes out. It all depends on how she remembers your last encounter. Karma's a bitch; a really hot bitch, but a bitch, nonetheless, and she NEVER forgets.

Chapter 5:
How Are You Going to Eat

I know it might sound weird, but sooner or later you will probably need to eat. Personally, I didn't eat for almost a year because I was a big fat bastard. I discovered that by almost completely substituting beer for food I was able to drop seventy unnecessary pounds dispelling the myth of the beer gut. Beer doesn't make you fat, it just makes you not give a shit what you shovel down your gullet at midnight. Personally, I never eat on an empty stomach.

[**food: something that nourishes, sustains**. Food, beer, same number of letters.]

Beer may sustain some, but there are those poor weak souls that require supplements. I found a couple of crafty little ways to make this possible without having to spend a dime and not even on purpose!

In 1998, I was on my fourth trip down the rabbit hole. I was living in Phoenix and wanted to move back to Illinois for no other reason than I was tired of construction. It wasn't a permanent move, it was more of a hiatus. The world was still turning at that time, so I didn't think it would be that tough.

[**hiatus: a break in continuity**]

I had lined myself up with a bartending gig at the Track Inn in Davis Junction when I made my final decision. That was a great job for three months, until it burned to the ground. That part sucked. No, I didn't do it!

After that, I moved in with my friend, Bob, who had a neat little cottage on the river. I tended bar here and there, but I wound up unemployed for a stint. Bob was a mechanic who was much in the same boat. He would fix a car once in a while in the garage at home but not often enough.

We managed to survive fairly well for a while until, one day, the pantry was completely empty. Not even the mice stuck around. I was broke at the time and he was suffering the same affliction. After sitting down at the table one night discussing our dilemma, Bob looked at me (not unlike a dog that had shit on the new carpet) and said, "I have a solution but you are going to owe me big— and you have to come with me."

Not having a clue where we were going, I jumped in the car and off we went. We ended up in his ex-wife's drive-way. "Oh dear God!" I thought to myself. "What in the hell are we doing here?"

Back then she was fostering around five kids and had government subsidies out the wazoo.

When we walked in she handed us grocery bags and said, "Take whatever you need, boys."

We went into the basement and I swear it was like walking into a commissary! We loaded up so much food we almost couldn't fit it all in the car.

There was enough food to last us six months and it did. He really bit the bullet on that one!

Way to take one for the team, Bobby.

If you don't have that option, then apply the same theory as *how acquire crap*. When people are relocating, they end up leaving all kinds of food in the kitchen. If you are willing to help them pack up the house, they will be more than happy to give you what's in the pantry.

In the two years I lived in "the cave" I did not go to the grocery store once. I made a point of it. An experiment, if you will. I wanted to see how far it would go. I made it two years! It was simply amazing. Not that I ever portrayed myself as a charity case. I wasn't and everyone knew that. I was simply still in a funk from the universe collapsing in on me.

After about a year or so in the cave, I started to run low on food. I really didn't care, but I thought maybe I should pretend to do something about it. Well, lo and behold, my favorite local bar, Aces and Eights, had become the next casualty of the economy. I had been going there for eight years solid and knew the owners really well. When it came time to pack the place up, of course, I was there. Honestly, not for any other reason than I wanted to help out and enjoy the final moments of my "office."

It took about a week to get everything into a storage unit. The fun part was I drank almost everything left in the place as we packed up. I like to call that my unwritten man law when helping anyone move: booze is an excellent lubricant/motivator when moving boxes.

More importantly, when we got to the walk-in cooler, I wound up taking nearly the entire contents home. Who doesn't love bar food? I mean really!

Well, there you go. Now I had food in the cave that would last for months! We had many a shindig with the usual suspects crashing in. It worked out well. I had the food and they brought the beer! I kept the pool in decent shape for the most part and it was good times. Good times.

As accustomed to having pockets full of money as I thought I had been previously, I found this time to be an unexpected surprise. Instead of being broke and miserable, I found I was enjoying myself. Instead of me footing the bill for the fun and games, it was happening all by itself.

The majority of the credit goes to a better philosophy on life. It turns out you don't need to have millions of dollars to have a good time after all. You just have to be the person others want to spend time with. Weird. Who knew?

Another fine moment in "J.T. magically winds up with a ton of food" history: check this out. True story, I swear. So there I was, going to bid a pretty big project, when, all of the sudden, the guy I was riding with started to run out of gas. We managed to coast into a gas station at the last moment. That didn't do us much good, as he had no cash on him and neither did I. Did I mention he was driving a 2005 BMW 720i? I thought that was the cute part. He had to call someone to bring some gas money, so we had to wait.

While we were waiting, a guy driving a sandwich truck was fueling up next to us. He looked over at me and said "Hey, it's the end of my shift and I have to get rid of these sandwiches. Do you want some?"

"Nah," I grumbled, "I don't have any cash."

"I didn't say buy. Do you want them?" he said.

"Well sure!" I spouted.

He opened the back of the truck and gave me five flats of the most kick ass sub sandwiches you've ever seen! When I got home, I threw them in the freezer. I had to eat the three that wouldn't fit. "Sub sandwich parties at J.T.'s house for a month! Bring beer!" The world turns in mysterious ways, I'll tell you. Mysterious, indeed.

If you keep your head up and explore your options with a trained eye, strange opportunities will present themselves. You just have to keep your eyes peeled if you're going to see that juicy banana.

Chapter 6:
How to Make Beer Materialize Out of Thin Air

[materialize: to appear especially suddenly]

Right out of the gate, I want to make something very clear: beer is your friend.

[friend: a favored companion attached to another by affection or esteem]

When you're happy, it puts a smile on your face. When you're sad, it's right there to cry with you. If you're angry, it will whisper confident nothings in your ear, giving you that extra bravado you'll need for a quality confrontation, and when you get your ass kicked, it's right there to ease the pain. How could you ask more of a friend than that? It's almost silly.

It doesn't have to be beer, per se. I drink beer at home, but when I'm out I prefer whiskey and diet coke. NOT Jack and diet. Jack and I had a knockdown, drag out brawl over two decades ago and I lost miserably. I can't stand the sight of that guy! Kessler is my spirit of choice. Smooth as silk. It says so on the bottle! Me and Julius have been pals ever since Jack did me wrong.

By the way, don't ever say that you can't mix your alcohol, or drink a specific kind of alcohol because it makes you crazy. That's the stupidest thing I've ever heard. The smell or sound of a particular kind of booze can trigger a memory of a crappy time you had once, but it's not what you drank, it's how much you drank! Alcohol is alcohol. The effect is the same regardless of the flavor.

How many times have you heard someone say (or said it yourself), "I can't drink tequila, it makes me an asshole!" No, you *are* an asshole! Booze simply puts you into focus for the rest of the world to see more clearly. If you're happy when you start drinking, you'll finish a fun person. If you're miserable at the beginning, you'll wind up crying and hugging everyone, telling them how much you love them.

An asshole that drinks becomes a bigger asshole. If you're an asshole in hiding when you start to drink, it's going to come out tenfold. If you are an asshole in hiding, I recommend you do not drink or the ruse will soon be revealed.

If you suspect someone of being an asshole in hiding, then feed them drinks. Your suspicions will soon be dispelled— or vindicated. I like to call it truth serum. Monitor your quantities, kids.

You don't need to be a raging alcoholic to appreciate a tasty beverage. Just enough to take the edge off is the proper dosage. Now every once in a while indulging in a feast of beer is bound to happen, and even still beer is there to bitch you out and make you feel like shit for taking advantage of it. Ah, what a good pal.

I'm only going to touch briefly on this subject as I've been informed that I need to devote my next "how to" guide to this very subject. It will be right after my "how to commit felony kidnapping and assault without having charges filed against you" guide. Yeah, I have that down pat, too, but that's another story and a damn funny one.

Making beer materialize before your very eyes is prestidigitation at its finest. I'm like the "David Copperfield" of beer. I have to tell you I truly have a rare gift in this department. It's almost creepy. Again, this is done unintentionally and with virtually no effort, yet it's been happening to me as long as I can remember. I don't know if I fully understand it myself, yet, but here are a few common denominators I can share with you.

It's good to have a local watering hole that you frequent. This is hopefully something you have previously established but, if not, you still got this. Get to know the patrons. There are a lot of cool and interesting people out there, so get to know them. I have heard some of the best stories about things you cannot imagine over a pint. I only wish I could remember half of them or wrote them down when they were fresh. When that book comes out, I *will* change the names to protect the guilty.

You also have to get to know the staff. Know the person serving you. It's cordial and don't be cheap. If you have ten dollars in your pocket, that equals two drinks and a two dollar tip, or three beers and a two fifty tip. Do your own math but remember, bartenders don't make shit by the hour.

Make sure you tip on the first drink. If you have that "I'll tip after I get good service" attitude then you will end up a thirsty soul for the night. Let them know you're not a cheap ass and they won't ignore you for half an hour. Call them by name when you see them and they'll remember what you're drinking without ever asking you again.

Become friends with the owners. It's just something that I have always done and when life goes askew it's a handy resource. Follow these simple rules at the pub and you'll be pleasantly surprised when the bartender gives you one on the house, just because. It can happen. I've seen it on TV.

Be someone that people can talk to. You don't have to dance naked on the pool table. In fact, that will probably get you eighty-sixed. Don't be the creepy guy at the end of the bar who doesn't talk to anyone and stares at other people's girlfriend's asses. That will get your ass beat and then even beer won't talk to you!

Here's a for instance. So there I sat, minding my own business, sipping my libation when out of nowhere this particular gentleman sat in the chair beside me. I had heard from others that he was somewhat of a grumpy fella, but I hadn't had the pleasure as of yet. Well, I generally like to be acquainted with someone before I decide if they're an asshole, so I struck up a conversation.

The next thing you know two hours had passed and every time his glass was empty he bought us a round and it was often. I thought perhaps I had met my nemesis. How could it be that another man could drink more than me? Poppycock! The game was afoot.

[**poppycock: empty talk, nonsense; origin: soft dung in Dutch dialect** or, as I like to call it, bullshit.]

We continued into the night and had a great time talking about all manner of things. I had finally gotten to the root of his disdain for the universe. As it happened, he had a multitude of health issues and his doctors told him they could do nothing to alleviate his condition. He was simply in a constant state of pain and discomfort. It turned out he wasn't an asshole at all. Lucky for me, because I think I had five bucks on me.

This very thing has happened to me repeatedly for decades, whether I've had cash in pocket or not. It didn't matter what part of the country I was in, either, and I've done some traveling, believe me.

I'll share with you my favorite Irish toast. I recite it often and nearly every time I do, another cocktail magically appears before me. "Raise your glasses! We've hardly had a drink all night. I'm not going to work tomorrow, I'm going to the pub instead. I've heard that work can kill a man, I'd rather be drunk than dead. *Slainte*!" As explained to me, the correct pronunciation is something like "Itsalawnchair" meaning to your health. That's a beauty bestowed upon me by my good friend John Windsor. *Slainte*, Johnny!

Chapter 7:
Women

Run. Run like the wind, Forest. Run like your ass is on fire!

[**run: to go without restraint, move freely at will**. Note, I didn't say where to run.]

I'd like to tell you that I have women all figured out and whatnot but no, not so much. "It's better to have loved and lost than never to have loved at all" my ass! What idiot came up with that one? I'll bet it was some dork that never had a girlfriend, ever. I say, "It's better to love them all and never to have lost at love." Not that I'm bitter, although I am the main ingredient in an Angostura Kiss. Google it. The drink dummy, not me! It's quite lovely.

All that aside, when you must dabble in the mine fields, use caution, for you are treading in barracuda infested waters.

[**mine: an abundant source**. Tricked ya!]

If you're in a predicament, the last thing you need is another mouth to feed drinks into. That is of course unless you can find someone who can support her own habits, like booze, cigarettes, or food. Even better if she can support yours for a while! Then, by all means, you have my blessing.

Ladies (if there are any of you reading this), I'll explain what I can for you, which isn't much. You don't have the same issues as we fine-feathered meat sticks have. I'm not saying one is worse than the other or that you're immune to a bizarre situation. I just don't understand you enough to offer any worthy advice. Sad, really, considering.

Not to toot my own horn or anything but throughout my escapades I've had far more than my fair share of trysts. I've known the company of well over a hundred women. That was hard to do considering I spent thirteen years of my life monogamously married, albeit, not in a row.

You would think with this amount of experience I would possess some concept of what's going on beneath those lovely, curly locks but, alas, it escapes me.

Use your best judgment, which probably isn't the best, and attempt to keep things short and sweet. This is not a time to cultivate a meaningful relationship. The shortest relationships I've had in my life are truly the most memorable; like the ones that lasted a week, or an afternoon, or that one time in the hot tub.

Here's a good tip. Look for someone who's from somewhere else and going back there soon. Make it unmistakably clear that it's just for a little while. Honesty is, without question, the best policy here. It's the best way to avoid those uncomfortable, awkward little bits in time. You know, like a long moment of silence, or a conversation. Be that strong, silent type and then ride off into the sunset and don't look back. Looking back shows weakness, or stupidity, or something. Don't forget your wallet on the nightstand. That would ruin the mystique.

In this way, that wonderful last memory she'll have will be of you and the great time she had. That way, there's a chance you can avoid having your eyes gouged out if she ever sees you again. "Oh, Suzy, do you remember What's-his-name I met last year? You know, for that one weekend? Oh, he was wonderful! I had such a great time! I hope I see him again someday. I wonder what he's doing now?" Yeah, be *that* guy.

So there I was, in the cave, living by myself at the time. My good friend Patrick was in town from Boston, accompanied by Dr. Beer. I love that guy's name. That's really his name. Huhuh... Doctor Beer...ahuhuhuh.

They met me at my "office" and we carried on as any good friends would that haven't seen each other for a while. At one point, Patrick asked me, "Do any single women ever come in this bar?"

"Nah, I never really saw any," I said.

What I had failed to realize was that I'd been married for the previous eight years that I had frequented the joint. I guess I just didn't pay attention before, because this time there was a hottie sitting right next to me, all by herself, and this time I was single. This time, I paid attention. With a little good old fashioned J.T. charm, she was naked in my pool within an hour. The boys still chuckle about that episode.

Lynn was a lot of fun. We really enjoyed each other's company. Really. It turned out she was leaving town for good in a couple of weeks. Her apartment was almost packed up already so she asked me if she could stay with me until she left. I had been alone long enough, and a limited engagement sounded like fun. How could I refuse?

When I got home from work every day for a week I was thrilled to find a pack of my cigarettes on the table, a twelve pack of beer in the fridge, and a naked, alluring temptress on the couch. We would make each other say "oooohh" for an hour or two and then I would cook us dinner. Boy, my life was just sooo terrible!!!

My "office" was only a six minute walk from the cave. We scampered down one Friday night and commenced to indulging in the local frivolity. When it came time to walk home Lynn had tripped on the curb and fell down. After assessing her to be sure she was uninjured, I suddenly had an epiphany. Right there before my eyes in the Target parking lot was a shopping cart. I picked her up and gently placed my precious cargo inside. We laughed all the way home. I got to live out an "Animal House" scene, except instead of ringing the doorbell and running down the street, I took her inside and had my way with her!

The next morning my daughter, Deborah, came over unannounced while we were frolicking on the couch. We sat up under a blanket, and Deborah said to me, "Hey, she's been here for like, a couple of weeks now. You guys aren't getting serious are you?" Before I could open my mouth to speak Lynn looked her in the eyes and said, "Oh no, honey, we're just using each other!" I couldn't have scripted a better line if I tried.

Lynn knew I was in no shape to carry on a relationship with anyone, and neither was she. We simply enjoyed our short time together and off to Oklahoma she went.

Hey, wait a minute. She's the one that rode off into the sunset leaving me with that wonderful last memory of her and the great time that I had! I didn't realize women knew how to play this game too! I told you I know nothing about women!

I had such a great time. I wonder if I'll ever see her again. I wonder what she's doing now. I hope her memories of me are as sentimental as mine are of her. She accidentally left her favorite pair of earrings behind. I was going to mail them off to her, but I got sidetracked and spaced it. When it finally came time to pack up the cave I picked them up and, without a second thought, I tossed them right into my "hope chest." When I open it again years from now and I pick up those earrings, I'll know in two seconds who they belong to, and a flood of fond memories will come gushing back to me. It's nice to have little mementos. I'm glad I kept them. She didn't forget her purse, or a wallet— a pair of earrings— perfectly executed. Pretty sneaky, sis.

This is the perfect sequence of events. Two people traversing different treacherous paths that stop to offer each other a moment of comfort, and then carry on their merry, separate ways. Nobody gets hurt, and good times are had by all. Karma's going to remember me favorably on that one.

I suppose I'm not saying you should hide from the opposite sex, just be sure to choose your opponents wisely, grasshopper.

[**opponent: one who takes the opposite position.** Ain't that the truth?]

Chapter 8:
How to Choose a Live-In

(Not a Wife. I'm a Tragic Failure at That)

I thought this subject needed to be addressed separately. I realize that some of you can't help yourselves, even though it may prove to be your downfall. I'll give you my thoughts on the matter, as I have meandered down this dusty trail myself a time or twelve.

When you find yourself with a pretty girl (or guy. I didn't forget you, ladies), the tendency is to want to have them around as much as possible. Not so much that you necessarily want to look at them twenty-four hours a day, but more so to ease your mind that they're not looking at someone else! With that said, I have a few criteria that should be met before this rash decision is cemented to the floor in the halls of epic tragedy.

Number one: said opponent better be hot, at least to you. Everyone has had a fling with someone that they're not particularly proud of.. That's not a bad thing, just don't let them move in. Chalk it up as experience and keep moving forward.

When the time comes that you do find someone that you find extremely physically attractive (because they usually don't find you), then make your move and record what transpires. Not on your iPhone, you literal meathead, mentally. Review the "mental" tape the next day and see how it went.

Did she have a good time, or was she just humoring you? Sometimes that's a hard one to distinguish, so don't be afraid to call witnesses if you have any.

The second thing you have to make sure of is that you had a good time. Don't be clouded by what you see. Remember, I don't care how hot she is, if she's single that means somebody else somewhere out there is sick of her shit.

Now that you have established that facts number one and two are positive, it's time for important fact number three. Is the person in question at least almost as amorous as you are? They don't have to be as horny as you, but a close second is a must.

If you find yourself sexually frustrated now, then just wait a few months living with the object of your wildest desires, and they won't give it up. You'll find yourself standing in the kitchen staring through the doorway into the living room at her lying on the couch and touching yourself in ways that would make your mother slap you. This is not only an unhealthy situation, it's a little creepy. These feelings must be mutual.

[feelings: the basic physical senses in which the skin contains the chief end organs and of which the sensations of touch and temperature are characteristic. Wow! That was deeper than I thought it would be!]

Case in point: there I was, living at my pal Bobby's place on the river in the late '90's when I landed a bartending gig at Slammers. (That wasn't a suggestive name for a bar, was it?)

Actually, the job found me. I was hanging out there for a few months, got to know the owner, Jeremy (as usual), and one night he asked me if I wanted the job. Sounded like a good idea so I took him up on it. It seems like every time I do that, something oddly magnificent comes out of it.

I had a nifty little trick I would pull every now and then. The bar had to close at one AM, due to state law, but that was about the time I wanted to play, so I would tell a select few patrons to go hide in the bathroom at twelve fify-five and then yell out, "Last call!"

After I shuffled everyone else out the door, I would lock it behind them and call out, "Ollyolly oxen free!" My special guests for the night would come back to the bar, and the carnage would ensue.

[**ollyolly oxen free: to indicate that players who are in hiding can come into the open without losing the game.** I like that one!]

One night while we were cavorting after hours, the music had stopped, so I went into the DJ booth to queue up another CD. When I pushed play on the disk player and turned around, standing before me was the pretty young thing I had included in the night's festivities, Nicole.

[**cavorting: to leap or dance about in a lively manner; to engage in extravagant behavior.** Yeah, all that!]

She was a beautiful little thing at five feet, three inches tall, maybe a hundred and five pounds, red hair and a lovely face with sparkling green eyes, and barely twenty one years old.

I didn't get a chance to say two words, and she had me in a lip lock. One smooth move deserved another, and before anyone knew what was going on we were naked and attacking each other.

[**attack: to set upon or work against forcefully.** Exactly. Now that's what I'm talking about!]

After about twenty minutes or two hours, it's hard to say, I said to her, "Oh shit. There's still a bunch of people at the bar!" I poked my head over the rail to look at the bar, and everyone who was supposed to be there had vanished. I told her, "Everyone seems to be gone. Why don't we go back to my place and finish what we've started?"

I locked up the bar and off to the house we went. Upon entering, we heard giggles coming from Bob's bedroom. In a quality ass/roommate maneuver, I threw open the door and Nicole and I burst into the room. On the bed in front of us was Bob with two naked strippers he had picked up from a club. The look on his face was priceless!!

"Get out!" he hollered and we ran to my room, laughing like little kids. A few hours later, Bob and his two guests burst into my room and Nicole, in mid stride and showing no signs of decelerating yelled, "Do you mind, I'm trying to finish here!" Out the door they went! We all laughed about that for years. By the way, she finished. It was the kind of thing dreams are made of..

Nicole didn't leave the house for a week. Seven, eight, nine times a day we would "consult the oracle." As much fun as the week had been, I cannot say that I was devastated to see her go. Not for any other reason than I needed to recuperate! I wasn't in the best shape of my life at the time and the girl damn near killed me! Men peak at eighteen and women peak in their thirties. This was a completely opposite situation. It's the kind of thing that heart attacks are made of..

Well, wherever she went she didn't stay long, because she was back in a week. Not a word was spoken. At least I have no recollection of talking about it but she moved right in. We enjoyed each other's company so much that it was an unspoken mutual understanding that she was just going to stay.

We spent days on end without ever getting dressed. An occasional break in the mêlée to stop and eat but not very often. I even went to the door with a sheet wrapped around me when the pizza guy showed up! It got to the point that I quit my job so I could spend more time in the bedroom! It was an unbelievable moment in history.

It wasn't purely copulation. We had a deeper connection than that. There were plenty of nights that we talked for hours on end and achieved a common mental ground that was very comforting.

I was still reeling over my divorce from ten years prior (I know, get over it) and she was doing much of the same with the freshness of her own. Just the same, we had discovered a way to forget about the universe and everyone in it. We had chemistry so volatile it would have killed the average alchemist. Good thing we were in the service industry!

A few months after she was there I discovered that my dog, Harley number one, a half Shepard, half Rott mix, was a jealous little bass turd. He would destroy the house at night because I wouldn't let him in my room with us, so one night when I knew Bob wouldn't be home until late, I locked the dog in my room, and Nicole and I commandeered the living room for the evening.

After several hours of reenacting a Barnum and Bailey production (just short of a trapeze), we curled up under a blanket on the floor to watch a movie.

Before the flick was over, Bob came home. His computer desk was in the living room close to where we were watching the T.V. and he sat down at the screen to do some web surfing.

Nicole had a sudden craving and slipped under the blanket. She was doing unspeakable things to me while I pretended to watch the movie, although it was quite impossible with my eyes rolled so far into the back of my head that I thought I could see Bob sitting right behind me!

Right before the moment of truth I felt a tap on my shoulder. Faster than I could turn my head a lit cigarette magically appeared beside my cheek! I snatched it and pulled a monster drag.

I have had a cigarette after such a moment an untold number of times, but that was the first and only) time I had smoked a cigarette during! You're a good pal, Bobby, a damn good pal.

Nicole stayed with me for two years. We were never officially "boyfriend and girlfriend." When I met her, she was a baby of twenty one years old, freshly divorced and had a very young son. I was thirty-something and had no plans for a life partner.

In '99 I moved back to Vegas and brought her with me. It didn't last long between us, and I put her on a plane to Chicago after a few months. This time I was sad to see her go, but the timing for us was not in the cards.

I thought about her often and hoped she was doing all right, but time moved on and I met someone else, Julie Ann. Nevertheless, Nicole never left my mind.

Have you ever had a nympho for a maniac? I don't mean for a weekend or a one-nighter but a lasting excursion? Ladies, you can put your hands down, there is no such animal as a male nympho and the female ones are so rare that it's like discovering a new polka dotted tree frog in the rain forest of the Amazon. Not unlike the polka dotted tree frog, it is a magical thing to behold. Two years together and the heat never subsided. I can't believe we didn't burn down a house or two hundred!

I did the math on it. Seven times a day was our average. Every day. Two years. I'm not talking about your five minute quickies here. It was an hour plus per session. Now, accounting for the occasional flu bug and leap year we still did it over five thousand times.

The fun part for me is the fact that she climaxed on average four times, each time. That's twenty thousand orgasms! Hard to believe neither of us died from dehydration alone! This was in the course of two years. Most people don't see that much action in a lifetime!

I like to think that although I'm no expert on women emotionally, I've got them pretty well figured out "motionally." If you can keep an actual nymphomaniac coming back for more for any length of time, it's an impressive entry on your resume. I'm just sayin'.

I ran into her over a decade later, when I was on my next hiatus. I didn't have any idea where she was or how to find her, but I remembered her father's name. It was a very standard Polish name, although not a standard name in English, therefore, I could not possibly forget it. I would tell you his name but then he would have to kill me.

He was in the phonebook, so I called and left a message with him to let her know that I was in town and to give me a call. She called me the very next day. We had a lot of catching up to do.

I was in Rockford and she was in Chicago, ninety miles away. Bob was getting married so she drove out for the wedding, and we spent the weekend together. I had nearly forgotten how much I missed her but she soon reminded me.

Me and that girl have something between us. I'm not even sure what it is but there is, but there's definitely something substantial. Who knows what the future holds for us. Who knows what the future holds for any of us. All I can say is time will tell, and time can't keep a secret for shit.

If you're going to move someone in, you better have real chemistry. If you don't, you're in for a terrible disappointment.

Chapter 9:
How to Find Work

Now it's time to get your ass to work. This is from a construction worker's point a view, but I'm sure the same principals apply, whatever your occupation. Before anything else, you have to be willing to work. That's half the battle.

I was out of work the last time because there wasn't any in my profession to be had. The time before was self-induced. The last time I had to diversify in order to find anything. No matter how diverse I tried to be, it was always the same genre, construction. That's not really diversifying, now is it?

I'll tell you that the best place to find work, and it doesn't matter what your skills are, is your local pub. If you followed my advice in Chapter 6, then you have a bigger network for potential employment than you think. As long as you followed the rules, then you have become a trusted member of the establishment. Whatever your skill is (hopefully you have one), if you let these people know what your profession is and that you're looking for work, chances are pretty good someone knows a guy who knows a guy who needs a guy that does what you do.

Even back in the long, long time ago I utilized this tactic. It not only works, but it gives you a great excuse to have a quality beverage. In the late '90's when I went to Illinois for a stint, I employed the same concept. It worked there just as well as anywhere else.

For eight years in the 2000's my "office" was Aces and Eights. I would meet my clients there to discuss their project. The pool table was a perfect plans desk to spread out the pages for review. If my cell battery was dead the phone would ring behind the bar for me. Everyone knew at the end of the day that, if my phone battery was dead, they could reach me at my "office". I would collect payments there, meet my subcontractors there, and on Friday all my guys would collect their paychecks there. I even sent and received my faxes there. All the patrons knew what I did for work and would tell anyone they knew that needed my services to call me. It was really cool. For Christmas, my partner, Gregg, and I would even hand out bonuses to our "clerical staff"— Ya know, the bartenders, waitresses and even the cooks. It was good stuff.

Once you establish a place as your "office," they will cash checks for you. That is really convenient. For the last twenty years, I have had a nice local pub for an office. Before Aces, it was Danny's II for a couple of years. I would cash small checks there because it was easier than hitting a bank first. One day I asked the manager if he could cash one for three thousand. He looked at me and said "J.T., for you I'll cash a check up to ten thousand before I ask questions." These were two party checks. When you pick up a check at six o'clock PM, and you need the dough that night, there is no other substitute for a bank than your office.

Before that, I worked out of Tommy Rockers for a few year, and before that, it was the Suburban West for a good seven years. Of course, I had a few satellite offices here and there, depending on what side of town I was working on, but I tried to stay true to my "main branch."

The monumental issue here is never bounce a check. I've had a few two party checks bounce over the years, but I got my ass straight to whoever wrote the damn thing the very next day and demanded cash, plus the bounced check fees. Upon returning to whichever "office" it bounced at, I would hand them the cash plus the additional bank fees. Never make your office pay for your customer's mistakes, and they will buy you a cocktail.

Even after the bubble burst and Aces closed, my next local pub, Decatur Tavern, became my best resource for finding the few small jobs I could get. I even ended up painting the owner's house! I was able to find Xander a gig there and, if all else failed, I didn't have far to go to drink away the anxiety of not finding anything to do.

"But if you're not working how could you afford to drink the anxiety away?" you ask. You obviously retained nothing from Chapter 6.

So, as I sat there one fine evening drinking away the day's angst, this particular fella sat down in the chair next to me. Turned out it was Stacie's cousin, Burke. We got to talking about my lack of work and how busy his warehouse was. He owned a plumbing warehouse in town and was not thrilled with some of the young bucks he had working for him. "Well, have I got just the nineteen year old buckaroo for you," I told him.

After much conversation and several cocktails, he turned to me and said, "If he's anything like you, then I just hired him, sight unseen."

I told him, "He better be like me, I raised him!"

Just like that my boy had a steady forty hours a week, plus overtime. That was perfect, because now he could start making payments to me for my crap he sold while I was in the pokey!

[**steady: firm in one's allegiance to someone or something.** That's perfect.]

The weird thing was that I hadn't seen Burke for nearly a year before this encounter. I saw him at my new "office" purely by happenstance. If I hadn't run into him when I did, who knows what my son would be doing now. He had been having a tough time finding anything steady for work, much like everyone else at the time. He loves his job and I'm happy for him. Again, I was at the pub for me, but by following the golden rule, I was able to help my son.

The best part is, he started paying me back from his first check and continued every payday thereafter. Turned out he was just like me and knows how to pay his debts. He has a firm grasp on what a bitch Karma can be.

He was on a good path and I was in the crapper, but he understands that things can change with the flip of a switch. There very well may come a time, I mean there *will* come a time when he needs a hand from the old man, and he appreciates what I do for him when I can. I love you, boy. Proud papa here.

The example goes to show it's not about construction work, necessarily, but work in general that you can discover if you talk to the people you're sitting next to with an honest aura.

[**honest aura: an energy field that is held to emanate from a living being free from fraud or deception.** It doesn't get clearer than that!]

There is no room for bullshit here. If you bullshit the wrong guy (or the right guy) one time you'll be blackballed for life, and news travels fast, my friend. Mighty fast indeed.

[**mighty: having great power or influence; towering over everything nearby**. People tend to overlook that part.]

In the toilet as I was, at least I still had my integrity.

[**integrity: incorruptibility**. That's me in a word, can't touch this.]

42

Chapter 10:
Don't "F" Yourself Up

[**fuck up: to ruin something by being stupid or careless.** Yeah, that's actually in the dictionary.]

There is one thing harder than plugging through this life with no money or job. Try to get it done when your body is severely damaged. An accident is just that, an accident, although the pain feels much worse when it happens due to your own stupidity.

[**stupidity: a quality or state resulting from unreasoned thinking or acting**]

When you're a young buckaroo you tend to heal pretty fast, or so I was led to believe. There are those precious moments in time when that's not so much the case. If you're going to play with fire, you'd better have a bucket of water nearby. As it turns out, health insurance is a damn fine thing to have when you tumble down the mountain. Literally.

So there I was, about twenty two years old, when my friend Matt said, "I'm going skiing this weekend, you want to come?"

"Sounds like a great idea!" I said. Oddly enough, not so magnificent this time.

It had been about eight years since I had skied. We got to Brianhead Mountain in Utah on a Friday afternoon. We skied into the night. It was probably seven thirty or so when Matt's phone rang. Someone in Vegas had died, and the wake was on Saturday, the very next morning. He looked at me and said, "I've got to drive back to town tonight, but I'll be back by tomorrow night. I need to make this last run down the mountain fast, so don't try to follow me! I'll see you at the cabin tomorrow." Well, because I was a genius, I deduced that if I went down the double black diamond trail I could beat him to the bottom by ten minutes. Bad idea.

Why is it always on the infamous "last run" of anything that you tend to do something incredibly stupid? I might as well have said, "Hey, y'all, watch this!" I've heard that's the last sound you hear before a Texan dies.

I made it about half way down when I tried to make a right cut off a mogul. Every part of my body executed a sharp right except for my right leg. It was still pointed left and showed no signs of following the rest of me. You would have thought my ski would have come off, but no, they were shitty rentals.

The most blood curdling "POP" you've ever heard echoed through the canyon. I flipped head over heels and as I was flying through the air upside down, I watched my leg flop about like a piece of overcooked linguini.

I landed in a heap of myself, unable to move. A pretty girl stopped to check on me and said, "I'm a nurse." She did a quick survey and said, "I'll get the ski patrol up here to get you, Don't move." That wasn't going to be a problem.

They showed up in minutes. One of the guys strapped a board to my leg, and they piled me in the sled. The guy in control squeezed the lever on the sled handle and said, "This is the brake: we can go as slow as you need to." "Screw that," I told him. "I look stupid enough as it is! Make this thing haul ass!"

He didn't hit the brake once, and I received resounding applause from the chair lifts! We flew down the mountain, to the convenient hospital at the bottom.

They threw me onto the slab on my back. The doctor raised my knee upward and pushed my foot close to my ass. He sat on my toes, got a firm grip on my calf and slowly began to pull towards himself. I watched my calf separate about half an inch from my thigh when I heard the doctor mutter, "EEWWW!"

I looked at him and said, "What the fuck do you mean EEWWW? You work in an E. R. at the bottom of a ski slope! You must have seen worse than this!"

"Nope," he said with absolute confidence. "You've completely ripped your ICL. You're gonna' need surgery immediately."

"How much is that gonna' cost?" I queried.

"About fifteen thousand, or so."

"SWEET!" I said. "You buyin', Doc?"

"Afraid not," he answered.

"Guess I'm gonna' limp!" I told him.

It took me almost a year to walk normally again. I lost everything I had and flopped on my mom's couch in Illinois while I healed. It was a humbling experience, to say the least.

The one thing I refused to do was limp. It was a long painful road, but I worked it and worked it until I managed to stop hobbling. Kinda' like losing my upper Michigan accent. "If yous guys work at somting hard enough, yah, yous can do anyting, eh?"

When I finally recuperated enough to work, I landed a bartending gig at Corey's Bluff. I had been hanging out there for a bit and the owner, Andie, who had become a friend of mine, hooked me up. I worked there long enough to scrape together the dough I needed to get back to Vegas and start company number three.

I had a trick knee that would twist out and leave me in horrid pain for days. One day when it went out on me the guy I was working with told me, "Dude, you have a trick knee!"

"What the hell does that mean?" I snapped.

"Lie on your back and give me your foot," he demanded. A little twist and a pull and the damn thing snapped right back into place like nothing had happened. No pain, no limp, no nothing.

"You gotta' be kiddin' me," I said. "I've spent days on end in crippling pain and that's all I had to do?"

"That's all," he said. Well, shit.

For about a year after that every time my knee would go out of place I would grab whoever was standing next to me and make them grab my foot, twist and pull, whether I knew them or not. It was ridiculous, but it got me through.

After a while, I figured out a way to do it myself. It got to the point where it would only go out once or twice a month, then once or twice a year, then not at all.

That was the first time I got a real taste of my own mortality. I've had a few heapings of it since. Not as yummy as one might think.

[Heaping 1: a collection of things thrown one on another : pile 2: a great number or large quantity : lot That suggests a bit more than a helping, no?]

It took many years for me to realize my leg was never going to be the same. No more acting like a moron. I eventually figured out that there are things I simply cannot do, like skiing or run a marathon, although I can still cut a mean rug better than most!

Eventually, my leg muscles had built up enough to compensate for the missing ligament and it no longer popped out. As long as I didn't do anything stupid, that is. I could lead a somewhat normal existence. The memory of the pain and suffering I endured defiantly keeps my inner dumbass at bay. Ligament, shmigament, they're overrated.

46

Dirt bikes, three wheelers, rock climbing, rappelling and cliff diving are still my favorite things to do, just with not so much reckless abandon as I have in the past. With age comes great wisdom— and caution— not sorrow.

Chapter 11:
Learn to Restrain Yourself

[**restrain: keep under control**. Good luck with that.]

It's not an easy thing to do to control one's irrational thoughts. Everyone has them. I don't care who you are. Learning to control their influence on your actions is the key. I can't say that it has always been my strong suit throughout the decades, but I have suffered the consequences enough times to offer some insight.

I'm certainly not saying "Don't take a risk." Life would be quite boring if you did that. Try to take calculated risks and you will have a much better outcome. Jumping off the bridge might sound like fun but if you don't check how deep the water is first you can get an unpleasant surprise.

There are occasions when you need to do something a little nutty, and not only for the pure enjoyment of it. Think of the stories you'll have. Life is something that is meant to entertain yourself and the masses. If you don't live it to the fullest, then you have wasted your time and that of others. You have to at least be able to tell a good story about it.

I have friends in Australia, Belgium, Montenegro, Korea, and points unknown, not to mention a few that have been on nearly every continent on the globe. I know for a fact that, at some point, everyone that knows me has told a story or ten about the wacky adventures they've had with ol' J.T. That makes me possibly the most world-famous man on the planet (or infamous, as it were) Six degrees of Kevin Bacon? I think it's more like three degrees of J.T.

The stories of your life are the things that define you. If you can't come up with any good ones, then look at what that has to say about you. Your stories are you. What you've done, where you've been, and the things that are yet to come if you are not afraid to take a chance. If you have nothing to talk about, then you are nothing. Get your ass out there and do something!

One of the best decisions of my life was a bit risky. I wasn't sure what the outcome was going to be, but I had a feeling it would work out for the best, and it did. It wasn't a rash decision. I calculated the risk and then I made it happen.

My wife Julie and I were sitting at home one weekend when her brother Rod called her and asked if we would stop by his girlfriend's house and check in on her kids. Rod and Nancy had gone away for the weekend and wanted to make sure her kids were being good.

Their father had passed away a couple of years prior, so they were home alone for the weekend. They were old enough to be alone for a couple of days, but they were also old enough to get into mischief.

We had never met them before. When we got to their house, I knocked on the door. Deborah opened it. We introduced ourselves, and walked staight into the house. I sat on the couch next to Deborah and watched the Food Network with her. We all hit it off well and talked for a while. She was thirteen, and her brother James was eleven, I think. Everything seemed fine, so we left after a bit and reported "all clear" to Nancy.

Rod and Nancy stopped going out after a short while but remained friends. We all hung out for the next couple of years.

When my family and I took weekend trips to the lake in the summer or the sand dunes in the winter, we would take the kids with us.

Two years later Nancy got pregnant by someone else. The baby was born premature (two pounds, nine ounces). Standard practice at the hospital for preemies was to administer a drug test to mom, which she failed. Deborah, at age sixteen, was wise beyond her years, knowing full well that Child Protective Services was going to send them all to foster care, so she ran away the day her mother went into labor.

Not wanting to see the kids separated, my wife and I went to family court and took temporary custody of all three of them. James was staying with his grandpa two blocks from us at first, but we had no idea where to find Deborah. Baby Laura was still in the hospital a month later.

I made a conscious decision not to inform the authorities that I couldn't find her. I had faith she would surface sooner or later. One afternoon out of the blue she called me. "Everything is fine," she said. "You don't have to worry about me."

I told her "I don't care what you tell me, I won't believe it till I see you. I don't care if you meet me at McDonalds or a frickin' gas station somewhere, I have to see you to believe you."

"OK, fine" she retorted. "I'll meet you somewhere tomorrow."

The next day I stayed home from work and waited for her to call. It was around noon when Julie and I were in the back yard. Deborah had walked through the house and out the back door. I looked up from the table, and there she was with a laundry basket in her arms.

"Can I stay with you guys?" she asked.

"Honey, I've had custody of you for months. Get your ass to your room." She had been living with a twenty-nine year old dirt bag for the few months she was gone. Being the overprotective dad guy I am, I really, really wanted to break his neck.

This was a time to truely exercise restraint. Julie told me, "If you beat him up, you'll drive her away. Let her figure it out on her own and she will appreciate you more in the end." That's exactly what I did, and he was out of the picture in no time.

[**appreciate: to grasp the nature, worth, quality or significance of.** Well, shit, that one made me feel good!]

Deborah was a little standoffish in the beginning. She wanted to handle her affairs on her own, and didn't want any help or interference from anyone.

I remember once Julie had asked her if she needed anything, "Socks, underwear, anything?"

"Don't buy me anything," she said. "I want to get a job and buy stuff myself."

I told her, "You have a full time job, kiddo. You're going to go back to school and finish it."

She had failed freshman year and had quit school altogether during her sophomore year. This was a very bright and intelligent girl, and I wanted her to reach her potential. I realized that the best way for this to happen was to get her into a new school where she didn't know anybody and wouldn't be distracted.

Another trip downtown and we got a zone variance to put her into a brand new school on the far north side of town. There was no bus to take her that far, and it was a pain in the ass driving her there and picking her up every day but it was worth every second of it.

Laura was released from the hospital when she hit six pounds. We had all three of them for several months, and we had a good time. It made me feel good to keep the family together.

Nancy did complete her court-ordered requirements around six months later. James and Laura, went home but Deborah wanted to stay with us. "You can stay here as long as you want, baby girl," I told her, and she did.

I remember our first Christmas together. She was still trying to be a tough girl and little Miss Independent. Then the week after Christmas we threw her a sweet seventeen birthday party. We all had a great time and after that the hard candy shell began to melt. Slowly but surely, she reverted to the sweet little girl that she had skipped over for a time. It was wonderful to watch the transformation.

By the next Christmas, little Miss "Don't Buy Me Anything" had a wish list longer than my arm. I loved it. It felt good to allow her a childhood, with her only responsibilities being to finish school and vacuum the carpet.

She finished school and graduated on time, without night school or summer school. I always knew she had the smarts for it, but she made it look effortless.

Deborah put herself through the Nevada Institute of Massage after high school and graduated near the top of her class. She has also made me a grandpa...twice. She has become one of the best decisions I've ever made. I'm not saying that I'm the best thing that could have happened to her. What I am saying is that she's one of the best things that ever happened to me. She's all growed up now but she still takes the time to come visit the old man. I love you, baby girl!

By the way, when she was sixteen she would pitch a fit when I would call her baby girl. One day she asked me "Why do you always call me that? I'm almost full grown!"

I told her "I don't care if you're forty-five, you'll always be my baby girl." She never questioned it again, and appreciates it more every day.

You all have a story to tell. I just hope for your sake it's an interesting one.

Chapter 12:
Learn How to Dance

First of all, it's something every man should know how to do. Why? Because, when you do it well, you exude confidence and complete control, even when everything else in your life seems completely out of it. The release and exhilaration you will feel is extraordinary.

Take a girl by the hand and explain which one is your lead hand. Then tell her, "Don't let go of it, or we'll all be killed." Now move to the rhythm, gently absorbing the melody. When the moment feels right, softly whisper casual instructions in her ear and begin to swing her around.

Always end the spin in an embrace, back to the "safe zone." The more you practice this, the more confident you will become, and the more confidence your partners will have in you. They have to trust you. I've always told my dance partners, "If I drop you, I will throw myself to the floor to break your fall."

Dance the first one slowly, so whoever you're dancing with can get a feel for where you're going. Then ask her for another go around when a faster tune comes along. Keep your movements as fluid as the nectar you're sipping.

Once you've become good enough, the girls in the room will begin to think of you as the most fun carnival ride they ever strapped into. I love the school girl giggles I hear when someone is having the time of her life.

When you can take someone you've never met before and float around the room as if you've done it together for years, it's a powerful feeling. Shock and awe will befall the room.

The bonus is that you get to meet beautiful women. Not just meet them but impress them with your style and grace. If you can guide a woman across a dance floor and keep your movements fluid and smooth, chances are it's going to go the same way behind closed doors. It's a great way to meet future opponents.

If she repeatedly steps on your toes, consider it a sign and move on to the next girl. Not every woman can dance, but if you can, then you will find that ninety-five percent of them can follow. You just have to know where you're leading them.

[**follow: to copy after, imitate**]

My favorite dance partners are the ones that proclaim they don't know how. Five minutes later, people think we've been married for ten years.

Don't pick the prettiest girl in the room on your first dance of the night. Pick the one that's having the most fun. I've found these girls to be the most willing to learn my simple steps. Once you've shown the room that you know what you're doing, everyone will want to play. Before long, they will be asking *you* to dance.

I'll pick anyone in the room. Big, little, young, old, scary, hairy, it doesn't matter. Once the music starts and we move together as one, it is a beautiful thing to experience.

I've always enjoyed watching couples that dance well together. When I was young I would think to myself, "I wanna move just like that." It's easier than you think. Don't be scared.

It's so much fun it's hard to describe. I especially enjoy taking the "seasoned" girls for a spin. You would be surprised how spry they can be. When the music is flowing, and the moves are smooth and eloquent, you can watch the spark in her eyes ignite to a burning flame.

[**seasoned: to make fit by experience**. I couldn't have said it better myself.]

You can almost see the memories of past lovers and good times roll through her mind. It's one of my favorite gifts that I love to give them (and receive from them).

When I was twenty one or so, I frequented Tiger's Pub. Every weekend the DJ, Mark, a good friend of mine, would spin records and the place was packed. Not CDs, mind you, actual licorice pizzas. I was one of those dummies that would say, "Oh, sorry, I don't dance," whenever a girl would ask me. I would play pool all night and hang with the crowd but never dance.

One fateful night these three black girls grabbed my arms and dragged me out to the floor. "Not like that, silly white boy, like this!" they scolded me. They taught me how to swing my hips like a wrecking ball. I had no idea what I was doing, but all of a sudden it hit me. You don't have to jump around like your pants are on fire. All you have to do is move to the rhythm. Duh!

That was it. I was hooked. I wish I could remember their names. Those girls changed my life. I made sure any time they came in that I would grab them and head to the dance floor.

I hardly ever played pool in that bar again. I found myself on the dance floor for five or six hours straight. I was in the best shape of my life, which was handy because it was this period that I found myself surrounded by more opponents than I could shake my stick at.. I developed quite the Casanovish reputation.

If you're feeling like your body could use some exercise, then get your ass on the dance floor. You'll probably feel like you're going to drop after the second song but if you keep it up every week, then soon enough no one will be able to keep up with you on the floor, or the bed, or what have you.

I could write a volume on Tiger's. Do you remember that scene in Dirty Dancing when Baby entered the room where the staff was partying and dancing nasty? It was just like that, I swear. Bumpin' and grindin' till the wee hours of the night.

I went there three nights a week for years. My friend Snuggles and I went there early one Friday right after my ski accident. His name was actually Dave. He was a six foot three, two hundred and fifty pound gorilla. He got the nickname Snuggles because he would pick guys up and crush them in a bear hug. The name stuck— kinda like every four hundred pound guy you ever met named Tiny. Anyway, I was in a leg brace from ass to ankle, and we were sitting at the bar enjoying a cocktail. Then the regular crowd started shuffling in.

"Hey, Dave, you see that girl? I took her home last week," I said. We continued sipping our beverages for a few minutes, and I said, "Oh look, I've been with that girl over there too." We had a little chuckle and reminisced over the crazy times we've had there.

Within the next hour, I was surrounded by over ten of my past liaisons. I began to feel a little awkward and said, "Given the shape I'm in, I think I need to hobble out of here!"

Out the door we sneaked, and took off laughing. What a good time that place had given me. I had more fun there than people should be allowed.

[**sneaked: undertaken or done so as to escape being observed or known by others**...and/or past opponents!]

I had to take a break for about a year and a half while my leg healed, but I wasn't going to let anything stop me from returning to the dance floor. I can still cut a mean rug today, and I do so as often as I can, which is at least a couple of times a week.

Last year I made a trip to Northern Michigan with my son, Xander. It was his second trip to the Upper Peninsula, but this time he was nineteen and old enough to retain a better appreciation for the region and the family we have there.

I had organized a little soirée at my mother's house. After dinner, my uncles, brother, and cousin started playing guitars and the girls were singing and dancing.

I grabbed my Aunt Janette, and we were flying around the room. She was an excellent dancer and we were spinning and twirling around just short of a back flip! When the music finally stopped we received cheers and accolades from the family. It was a wonderful time.

My favorite moment was when I looked at my boy. The expression on his face was that of pure amazement/disbelief. I could hear what he was thinking, "Holy crap! People really do this kinda stuff?" Yes, my dear boy, people really do this kinda stuff. We had us a good old fashioned hootenanny.

[**hootenanny: a gathering at which folksingers entertain, often with the audience joining in**. When's the last time you did that?]

It was a great time with or without the dance but with it made for a fantastic memory. I shan't forget it...ever, and neither will Xander. I've taught him many things over the years. I think it's time to teach my boy to dance.

Chapter 13:
Be a Romantic Sap

(It's Good for You, Like Orange Juice or Spinach)

[**romantic: marked by the imaginative or emotional appeal of what is heroic, adventurous, remote, mysterious, or idealized**. Wow, that!]

[**sap: a watery solution that circulates through a plant's vascular system; a body fluid (as blood) essential for life, health, or vigor; a foolish gullible person**]

[J.T.'s interpretation of romantic sap: a foolish, gullible solution marked by the imaginative or emotional appeal of what is heroic, adventurous, remote, mysterious or idealized that circulates through a vascular system essential for life, health, or vigor. There is no imaginative or emotional system without a heart and a solution.]

Some people out there have no romance in their life. It crushes me up inside.

Romance is something that can get you through the day when things aren't going as well as expected. You have to have it on your mind the whole day in order for it to come to fruition.

The thought of how your actions will drive someone wild will preoccupy your mind all day, shedding a different light on everything. Think of the sappiest thing you can do to make your significant other melt and the payoff is astronomical. A little bit goes a long way, but none at all will leave you out standing in your field...by yourself.

Hopefully your opponent will reciprocate. It will start to lose its luster if it's always one-sided. If your significant other doesn't have the imagination to "wow" you every now and again, then you're probably with the wrong person.

It doesn't have to be every single day. That would make it mundane. When it's least expected is when it's most effective. I don't know how some people stick together for years with no fire. When the fire is gone, I'm gone with it.

Pick her some flowers. It's not about spending a bundle of money. It's more heartfelt when you take the time to pick your own bundle. Leave little notes around the house, ones that she won't find until hours after you've left the house. If you're really sappy, it'll take her days or even weeks to stumble across them. The little things like that show her you care and you're thinking about her.

My second wife was completely surprised when I asked her to marry me. We were on the dance floor (shocker) when I whispered in her ear, "Baby, I've been keeping a secret from you... I want you to be my wife." I think she cried for an hour. When she could finally speak again, she asked me to set a date. I said, "How about in a couple of months. I was thinking March ninth, the day of our first kiss two years ago." She didn't see that one coming! She cried for another hour. Believe it or not, I actually remembered.

I'll never forget that night we kissed. My partner, Gregg, and I had rented a limo bus for the night. We had a bunch of friends from in town and a handful from Illinois that flew in for the ride. We hit every casino in town. By four in the morning, Julie and I were the last two in the limo. I take that back. My nephew, Aaron, was still there, but he was passed out on the floor.

Julie was napping on the bench with her head in my lap. I woke her softly and with my finger gently coaxing her toward my lips, I whispered, "Hey Julie, come here."

She leaned up to me and we kissed passionately for the rest of the trip home.

The next day, Julie called her sister-in-law, Kat, who was married to Snuggles. Did I mention Snuggles was Julie's brother? She had heard many a story about Mister Casanova and was feeling a little embarrassed.

I had known Kat for a decade. Now you can imagine the stories Julie had heard about *this* guy. Well, her first words to Kat were, "Oh my God, Kathy! I kissed him!" Kat calmly replied, "That's OK honey, so did I." I had chased after Kat ten years prior! Julie's jaw hit the floor!

Kat and I would dance the night away back in those days. I was putting the moves on her for a couple of days and one night Dave sat next to me at Tiger's and calmly said, "J.T., I know you're after her, but me and Kathy have been secretly dating for weeks now. Would you please stop chasing her?"

"Holy crap, Dave!" I belted. "I had no idea. There's plenty of fish in this barrel. No problem dude!"

I was blown away. This was a gorilla that could have crushed me like a grape and, instead, he asked me "please!" I never saw that coming. It was easy for me to move on because, at the time, I wasn't looking for a relationship with anyone anyway. It wasn't until ten years later that the Trojan horse of marriage came a'knockin'.

The morning after Julie and I consummated our relationship, I called Dave on his cell and said, "Hey dude!! I got lucky last night...with your sister!" I figured he'd find out sooner or later, so it might as well have come from the horse's ass! At least I had enough sense to tell him via cell phone! That made it hard for him to crush me!

He was a little hot at first but once I convinced him that I really liked her he calmed down. I truly did.

I've always been good at getting the girl, just not so great at keeping her. Julie and I had eight good years together, by far my longest run at it. When it came to an end, I was still deeply in love with her but the flame had extinguished. I suppose I'm as much to blame as her. *C' est la vie.*

    [*c'est la vie*: **that's life;** that's how things happen. What can you do?]

Chapter 14:
Limit the Bullshit around You

There's always going to be some degree of bovine fecal matter in your life. It's inescapable.

The best you can shoot for is to limit it to the smallest possible pie. Your brain will thank you for it. If, for some reason, you find yourself happy floating around in it, then I'll digress. There are those that feed off of it. Personally, I frown on picking it out of my teeth.

If you have coworkers, neighbors, or family members that never stop bitching or crying, then ignore them. If they don't get the hint, get rid of them. If they won't quit or you can't fire them, then find a new job yourself. Move out of state if need be. You can't go on day by year putting yourself through such turmoil. It's not conducive to a healthy attitude.

You have to be able to separate yourself from a situation that you have no control over.

The last thing you need is to get wrapped up in someone else's bullshit. Chances are you have enough of your own. The trick is to use discretion when choosing who you spend your time and energy on.

When I was a kid someone told one of the most important personality quirks of the human animal. I can't remember who said it, but it was probably my mother. Thirty plus years later and it's still in my head. "You are who you hang with." People have a tendency to become the person they spend the most time with, whether on purpose or not. That whole birds of a feather thing, guilty by association, and whatnot.

You have two choices. Either become them, or make them become you. If you're a worthy human being, then I suggest the latter. There are more sheeple out there that need guidance than you realize. I've witnessed terrible choices made by others and wish I could have intervened more than I did before it was too late.

[worthy: having sufficient value or importance; honorable]

I've done the best I know how to help those along the path and tried to make a difference whenever I could. Sometimes there's nothing you can do. Alas, there are those that just don't listen.

If, by chance, you find that you have trouble making the right decisions, then you want to be the former. The hard part is to recognize who is worthy to hang with and who will drag you into the mud with them.

It's not a bad thing to play second fiddle if the first chair is a virtuoso. What would Batman be without Robin? A dark and lonely knight, that's what. Everyone needs companionship, the leaders, the followers, and those in between.

[virtuoso: a person who has great skill at some endeavor. Whatever it may be...]

I like to think of myself as somewhere in the middle. I consider myself as somewhat worthy and try to surround myself with others of even greater worth. It's helped me to become a better person in the long run.

If bad things are happening all around you and you do not possess the strength to ward it off, then you are doomed to replicate. Don't replicate bad behavior, emulate good behavior.

[emulate: to strive to equal or excel]

Your life will be much more satisfying in the later years. It doesn't happen overnight. Be patient.

When I started business number one in '89, I was having a little trouble knowing how much to charge my clients. I also was worried about length of time before billing, materials, and keeping my books straight.

I asked my supervisor, Dimitris, at my day job what he thought about my concerns and he told me, "Don't worry about the details, just do the right thing, and the money will follow." That was an answer I didn't expect. I was waiting for a string of crap that I was to follow. Instead, that's all I got. It put me into a completely different mindset.

[**right: being in accordance with what is just, good, or proper**. Now that makes it easier to understand my point, doesn't it?]

I applied this philosophical quip for the next twenty years. I think he's half the reason I was as successful as I was for so many years.

"Just do the right thing. The money will follow."

Ah, but what is the right thing? That is the question, isn't it? The way I took his advice was not just a matter of avoiding mistakes. I'm talking about cooking pancakes when you're told to make waffles. That would be a mistake. Everyone makes mistakes.

I took the right thing as a morality issue. Don't be greedy, don't be a cheat, do the job at hand to the best of your abilities and don't be an asshole. That's the right thing and, magically enough, the money came pouring in for decades.

Despite the crappy way things have turned these last couple of years, I'm not swayed from my basic philosophies. Things are not just bad for me. Everyone is having a tough time of it.

When the day comes that the world economy (my favorite four letter word) turns for the better, I'll be back on top. It's strictly a matter of survival until then. I got this. Can't scare me. I'm fearless.

Chapter 15:
Keep a Cool Head

Everyone who has ever taken a breath has had a moment of crisis. The key to surviving it: Don't toss your cookies over spilt milk. Panic will only cause a riot. Get a grip on the mop and clean it up. There's plenty of time for a panic attack after the situation has been rectified.

[crisis: the decisive moment; a situation that has reached a critical phase. I'll say it did. **]**

There's only one thing worse than having a lighter and no cigarettes. That's having a cigarette with no light. Always be prepared.

Know what to expect before you get yourself into a situation and be ready to deal with the worst possible outcome. You never know when disaster will strike. It helps to have the necessary tools at arm's length, just in case.

So there we were, cruising across the lake, when all of the sudden from out of seemingly nowhere, I leaned to my wife and said, "Hey honey, look at the pretty white caps!" I think you can see where this is goin'...another "hey, y'all, watch this!" moment.

Myself, Julie, Xander (who was 12 at the time), and my friend, el Gato were out having a great weekend at Lake Mead. When it came time to head back to the marina, the sky was blue, the temperature was moderate, and we were enjoying the soft breeze that was beginning to stir the spring air.

El Gato is a good old fashioned, white boy from Texas. When we would go to Tiger's pub, Mark the DJ would call him Tommy the Cat. Tom and I had worked on the same job sites together for years. Often there were many Mexicans working there, and when I spoke to them, I would refer to Tom as Thomas el Gato. Years later it got shortened, but it stuck. I still call him el Gato today, twenty years later.

We were headed south entering Boulder basin, which was the broadest section of the lake. The headwind was increasing by the minute and, before I knew it, we were in a shoving match with eight foot swells, getting bigger by the moment. The white caps weren't so pretty anymore.

We were about halfway across the basin before I began to realize we could possibly be in a pickle. I kept thinking to myself, "It's no big deal. This boat can handle it."

I had a 1968 twenty-six foot Chris Craft cabin cruiser with a ten foot beam. It slept six comfortably, had a small galley, head, and even a shower. This vessel was off-shore worthy, there was no doubt in my mind. How could a puny lake cause me any grief, even if it is the largest manmade lake in the United States? It had a three-eighteen gasoline powered inboard V-8 engine with a two-speed stern drive and a rudder as big as my fat head. "Give me your best shot, lake!" I taunted. In retrospect, I probably shouldn't have made that dare.

The ride was getting pretty rough, but I kept the bow pointed straight into the wind. As a precautionary measure, I calmly called out a command to the crew, "Everyone needs to put on their life jacket." Julie's face turned as white as my ass. I could hear her thinking, "Oh God! If J.T. says put on a life jacket, then we're all going to be brutally slain!" That was pretty much the consensus of the entire crew.

My Uncle Bob was Commander of the Coast Guard Auxiliary on Lake Superior and he not so jokingly would say, "That's not a life-preserver, it's a floatation device— So we can recover your body." Everyone on board had heard me tell that story before.

With each giant wave, I gunned the engine and climbed to the crest. Peaking over the top, I backed off the throttle, teetered over the edge and coasted down the back side. With each ascent, I found myself having visions of The PerfectStorm, but it seemed to be going swimmingly.

Or so I thought...

Just as I was about to reach the summit of the next mountain top a gale force rogue gust came at us from the west. I counter steered to the right to try to compensate, but the vessel was turning to port, despite my efforts. My expert mariner alter ego convinced me, "If I give it full throttle and crank the helm to starboard, the boat should be able to make the turn back into the wind, and I'll crest the next wave at a perpendicular angle." Another brilliant idea.

[**gale: a wind from thirty two to sixty three miles an hour.** Closer to the sixty three side, trust me.]

We crested the next wave all right, at a forty-five degree angle and full throttle. The only thing missing was the Dukes of Hazard musical horn you heard every time those crazy Duke boys launched the General Lee over Choctaw Ridge.

Do you understand how a swell works? I do...now. If you encounter a five-foot wave, behind it, the water recedes five feet, leaving a ten foot deficit from top to bottom before the next wall comes at you.

I launched that massive beast off the top, wide open, and by the time we came down my landing ramp had left without us. The boat plummeted ten feet and slammed into the water, like a brick on an eggplant. Within three seconds, the next wave hit, except this time we were parallel to a ten foot wall that toppled over us.

It struck the starboard with an evil grin and rocked us almost completely over. I was clinging onto the side of the boat, like a spider monkey while my feet were dangling over the chairs! Luckily the crew was down below.

It struck us hard and turned us over so far that all of the oil in the bottom of the engine block flooded the top of it, causing it to belch out a thick plume of blue asphyxiating, smoke that filled the cabin and killed the engine.

The ship was awash with panic. I told everyone to brace themselves for the next hit. We clutched the sides and prepared for the worst. The next one came but with no vengeful white cap. We pitched this way and yawed that, but we rolled with it, apparently out of imminent danger, although we were dead in the water with smoke rolling out of the cabin like a deleted scene from a Cheech and Chong flick.

Just as I turned to the aft, I saw Julie with a death grip on the shoulder straps of Xander's life jacket, preparing to eject him overboard. "Stop!" I screamed. "The ship hasn't gone down yet! Get a hold of yourself!" I began coolly barking orders.

"Xander, secure the gear below! Julie, lash the doors and help the boy! Gato. let's open the hatch and get this pig started!"

I honestly had no clue what the hell I was doing. In an attempt to avert mass hysteria, I thought that by keeping the crew busy doing seemingly important shit, perhaps I could avoid a full scale mutiny.

El Gato and I wrenched open the hatch. Luckily I had a can of ether in the engine compartment. I gave the carburetor a healthy squirt. Room, room, room, room, vvrooooom! What seemed like half an hour was actually more like five minutes and just like that, we were under power again.

I swung her about and put the wind at my back. This time, when I crested a wave, I eased off the throttle, just enough to stay on top of it. I was going with it instead of trying to fight against it, and we rode that wave like a giant surfboard. I was finally able to maneuver close enough to shore and ducked into a hidden cove protected from the elements, where I dropped anchor.

It only took an hour for the freak windstorm to subside. We turned back towards the marina and steamed ahead. An hour later we were safely back in the slip enjoying a well-deserved cocktail, all souls present and accounted for.

If not for the courage (or stupidity) of this fearless captain, the little ship probably wouldn't have been in that predicament in the first place but by staying cool and having the necessary emergency supplies onboard (ether...also handy for kidnapping), I was able to escape disaster.

I didn't have my panic attack until five hours later when I was in the privacy of my master bathroom. As I took a shower one thought kept ricocheting inside my head like a racquetball. "Pitch him off the back of the boat? Really?" Some folks are just not equipped to handle a crisis.

Don't be *that* guy.

[**equipped: furnished for service or action by appropriate provisioning**. Now read that sentence again with the definitions instead of the words and it's a whole lot thicker! "Some folks are just not furnished for service or action by appropriate provisioning to handle a decisive moment that has reached a critical phase." See what I'm gettin' at?]

Chapter 16:
Get Out of the House

You need to exit the cabin and do something once and a while. Not working and having little money is no excuse to lock yourself up and hide from the world. That won't solve anything.

Wherever you live, there's bound to be something going on somewhere that won't cost you an arm and a leg. Don't be a bird trapped in your own cage.

Every town has some sort of newsletter (usually free) on the stand at your corner convenience store or the cigarette machine at the pub that tells all about local events. Little shows like this are usually quite entertaining, and free, or at least damn close to it.

You'll hear music you probably never would otherwise. It's a good thing to experience new and different sounds. Music is the gateway to the soul.

[music: the science or art of ordering tones or sounds in succession, in combination, and in temporal relationships to produce a composition having unity and continuity. "There is a music for everybody"—Eric Salzman, an American composer, author, impresario, music critic, and record producer. Well stated Eric.]

I think I was seven or eight when I heard my first concert. I was in Ontonagon, Michigan, and we went to a hootenanny, a real big one downtown at the local theatre. I can remember all sorts of different music echoing off the walls of the place, but nothing struck me.

My cousin Ricky was in the show that night. He had a band at the time. They went on stage in full makeup and did a Kiss tribute. It was awesome. I loved every bit of it. That was the start of it.

Then it happened. I don't remember the name of the band onstage, but I do remember what song they did, a cover of Styx "Come Sail Away." My mind was blown away. The melody, the lyrics, the beat, everything about the song just sucked me in. I mean come on, they were really singing about aliens? How cool is that to an eight year old?

That was the first time I was truly touched by music. It shaped my musical taste for the next thirty-five years. I realize the song might be a little stale for some, but if it came on the radio right now I would stop typing, close my eyes, and immerse myself in the memory.

I remember that moment, and the feeling, like it was ten minutes ago. It may have been a long time ago, but it's something that will stay with me forever.

When it comes to music, don't listen to what all the cool kids are playing. Listen to whatever it is that moves you. If you don't really feel it, then you're faking it. There are too many genres out there. Something is bound to give you that funny feeling. When you're touched by the right melody, it's like having your first orgasm, and you'll never forget it.

A few years ago, when my boy was sixteen, I took him to see Asia and Yes. Tickets were like twenty bucks apeice. Asia opened with their standard hits and then moved on to their more obscure stuff. The whole time I was watching my teenage son sing all the words to this early eighties band, and we were having a great time.

Then toward the end of their set, Asia busted out with "In the Court of the Crimson King," a cover of none other than King Crimson. Once again my son knew all the words. I had forgotten most of them myself! He had learned it on his own because it moved him. I taught him well! It was a very proud moment.

I never forced my flavor of music on him. I had a collection of twenty eight thousand songs, or so, on my computer at home and had it plugged into an equalizer, three amplifiers, and eighteen speakers. I simply made it available to him and gave him the right to like it or not.

Turned out, he liked it. Who wouldn't, honestly? Pink Floyd, Jim Morrison, Porcupine Tree, Radiohead, Hoyt Axton, Jerry Jeff Walker, the Posies, the Refreshments, School of Fish, Dada, Ghost of an American Airman, Josh Clayton Felt, Alexi Murdock. That is but a fraction of the stuff I have gathered and grown to love. You cannot imagine my eclectic music collection. YouTube some of it, if you can find it!

Then Yes took the stage. Steve Howe never left his stance and played double duty that night on lead guitar. They played to perfection even though John Anderson was absent due to throat issues. The replacement singer was some guy the band found on YouTube, and he was great! Who would've thought?

A good concert can give you something to talk about for years to come. If you're lucky, it'll give you something to talk about for the rest of your life.

There's plenty of other ways to entertain yourself without spending a bunch of dough.

Go to the lake, river, pond, or whatever. Enjoy the wonders of nature and bring a friend to share it. It's only half the fun if no one else can remember the adventure and share stories about it.

When I was eighteen in Illinois, we had a rock quarry that hit a spring and flooded the bottom. We used to ride our motorcycles out there, hide them in the corn field, and jump off the cliffs. There was a twenty footer, a thirty-five footer, and a sixty footer. It took me a couple of months to build up to it but, eventually, I mustered the courage to dive head first off the sixty footer. What a rush!

I didn't take any kind of drugs in those days. I didn't need 'em. There was just no substitute for adrenaline.

Right next to that quarry was another pit that had hit water. We measured it with a rope. This one was a ninety foot drop! We climbed to the bottom and jumped in the water to investigate the depth. It was plenty deep enough with no obstructions, so we climbed back to the top to see who had the nards to jump!

My friend, Russ, and I stood about fifteen feet from the edge. "You go left, and I'll go right," I instructed. "One, two, THREE!" We ran our hearts out. The only way to make sure no one chickened out was to run so fast there would be no time to turn back!

Russ and I left the comfort of solid ground under our feet simultaneously. As we dropped through the air all you could hear was "AAAAAHHH!— (giant gasp of air)— AAAAAAHHHH!" SPLASH! That's right, it was a "two screamer." It seemed like an eternity had passed before we broke the surface of the water. That was, by far, my ultimate rush. I had it on video for years but eventually lost it. Perhaps it's time to get on a plane and do it again.

This weekend, for instance, I'm going on a dirt bike ride. It's a ride we used to do annually for seven years, but I haven't had the money for it in the last three. I'm just going to make it happen, whether I have the money or not. It's therapeutic and necessary.

Twenty bucks for gas, twenty bucks for the hotel room, and twenty bucks for the bar once we reach our destination. I can make that happen if I have to borrow it.

The trip begins in Moapa Valley, just outside of Vegas. We follow the railroad tracks for a mile or two, then we hit the offroad trails through the mountainous desert -- only following the tracks a couple more times in order to traverse some otherwise impassable cliffs and whatnot.

Ninety miles north we'll hit Caliente, a sleepy little desert town in the middle of nowhere. After rolling down Main Street on quads and dirt bikes, we'll stop at the hotel, chain our bikes to a light pole, and walk a half a block to the Knotty Pine for refreshments and mayhem. The next morning, a quick pit stop at the gas station and then hit the trail back to Moapa.

It's an awesome trail and a much needed stress release valve. It's ninety miles one way. We have made this trip a dozen times over the years, but there was one trip in particular that caused more stress than it cured.

So there we were, fifty miles from nowhere, when all of a sudden the trail beside the tracks was blocked. "We're going to have to pop over the tracks, get past the blockade, and pop back onto the trail. No sweat," or so I thought.

Tommy's dad, Pops, was on the ride with us. He was not a seasoned veteran of the trail and he was riding a quad that he had borrowed from my friend, Steve. He was unsure about how to cross over a set of train tracks.

Everyone else had crossed over first and made it back to the trail no problem. Pops was the last to go. I had gotten off my quad and positioned myself behind him as a spotter in case trouble brewed.

Pops had gotten his two right tires over the first rail and headed north, straddling it, which was just enough to get him past the barricade. When it came time for him to return to the trail, he turned the wheels to the left too slowly. By the time the right front tire made contact with the rail, he didn't have enough momentum to bounce over it. No matter how much throttle he dug into, the bike just slid along the rail and continued north.

I suppose you can probably guess the next sound we all heard. "WOOOO WOOOOO!" Oh yeah. Around the bend up ahead, less than half a mile away, came the freight liner, locked in a head on collision course with Pops and closing fast.

Tommy and I ran for the ass end of the quad. "This won't be hard" I kept thinking out loud. "We'll just grab the back rack and flip the damn thing over onto the trail, Pops and all."

Like a bad movie, arms outstretched, running at top speed, we were seconds from grabbing the rack when the unthinkable happened. Pops hit the gas. "NOOO!" Tom and I screamed as he picked up speed, blundering into an inevitable head on collision with the Union Pacific like a slot car, incapable of changing direction!

All we could do was stand and watch, our eyes transfixed on the horror, unable to turn away. Ya' know, like watching a train wreck!

At the last possible moment, I yelled at the top of my lungs "Pops! Let it go!" He was obviously so concerned about wrecking a bike he had borrowed that he was going to save it, no matter what, but I must have gotten through because two seconds before impact he ejected himself off the quad and rolled into the trail...SLAAMMM!

The train smashed into the bike with the horrendous crunch of twisting metal. There was a five gallon gas can strapped to the front rack, and it spewed everywhere upon impact. Tom and I were fifty feet away and running from the tracks to avoid being hit by debris. When the gas can burst open, it splashed both of us with gasoline. Thank goodness there was no spark, or we would have been running torches!!

The next sound we heard was predictable: "EEEEEEEEEEEE!" The rest of our crew was a half mile ahead under a bridge when they heard the train hit the brakes. "Uh, oh, that's not a good sign!" they thought and came riding back.

It took the train half a mile to come to a screeching halt. We rode up to the engine, and as we approached it, the engineer swung the door open and yelled to us, "Did he make it?" Pops had come so close to being splattered like the gas can that the engineer didn't see him jump off at the last second, due to the height of the locomotive.

"He's OK!" I answered. It was obvious the poor engineer was shaken but, as he explained to us, it wasn't the first time he'd seen it happen and not always with our happy outcome.

"You guys better disappear. The railroad investigators are on their way, and you don't want to be around when they get here," he told us. What a cool guy!

Steve had just bought the quad that was mangled under the train, and he refused to give it up. We borrowed a giant crowbar from the rail workers and managed to dislodge the crumpled hulk. After tossing it in the bushes, we beat feet back to the trail and vanished before the fuzz arrived.

On the trip back to Moapa the next day we found it. Upon further inspection, only the front end was destroyed. The engine and rear of the quad were still intact. Steve desperately wanted to bring it home, but how?

"I've got it!" I snorted. "Someone give me a hand." I was riding a Honda utility quad that I had borrowed from my friend, Shawn. We picked up the front end of Steve's quad, set the crumpled mess on the rear rack of my ride and strapped it down.

I was able to piggyback it the fifty miles back to our trailers.

The only hard part was I couldn't make any sharp turns because I had so much weight on the ass end of my quad. Every time I tried to turn the handlebars the damn thing just kept going straight!

We all made it back in one piece. The memories of that trip will last me a lifetime. I'm glad I got out of the house on that day. What a story I got out of that one! If you don't get out of the cabin, you'll have nothing to talk about, except for cabin fever, and that's not fun.

Chapter 17:
Get a Second Opinion

If someone gives you news that you don't want to hear, then get a second opinion. There is no rule that says the first guy is always right. That doesn't mean you're home free but at least there's a chance the first guy was just an idiot.

There's plenty of room out there for individual opinions. They're kinda like assholes. Everybody's got one, and they're usually full of shit. Don't base your future on just one.

It was around 2001. Xander had gone to visit his biological father for the summer up north. Julie and I were having fun with our short freedom and were using it up to the best of its potential when the call came in.

It was Julie's ex calling to inform her that Alexander was in the hospital. He was having trouble seeing anything, and the doctors were running tests on him trying to figure out why.

The next call was a complete nightmare. The doctors hypothesized that he had a parasite that had burrowed into his eye and was traveling to his brain. They gave him a year to live. The boy was eight.

You cannot imagine the hysteria. Julie completely lost her mind. It took me days to calm her down enough to speak. All I could tell her was to stay calm until we got him home, and we would take him to a specialist in Vegas. I told her that I didn't believe any of it until I heard it from seventeen different doctors.

We got him home a couple of days later and took him to see a retinal specialist. He performed numerous tests on him and then all we could do was wait.

The diagnosis came back with mixed reviews. Multi-focal choroiditis, a chronic disease, to be sure. The prognosis was that he will eventually be blind. Probably by the age of twenty, but at least he's not going to die from it like idiot number one had deduced.

[multifocalchoroiditis: the word you've entered isn't in the regular or medical dictionary.]

[Wikipedia footnote-Multifocal Choroiditis (MFC): The fundus presents with yellow or gray lesions (white dots) at the level of the choroid and RPE. The size of the white dots are between 50 to 500 micrometres and localized in the macula. MFC is characterized by vitritis and anterior chamber inflammation. Decreased vision due to vitreous inflammation may occur. Unlike MEWDS, MFC is a chronic disorder and macular scarring contributes to severe visual loss. Theories regarding the cause include "an exogenous pathogen sensitizing an individual to antigens within photoreceptors, RPE, or choroid."]

[J.T.'s pieced together definition: inflammation and bursting of the vascular membrane containing large branched pigment cells that lie between the retina and the sclera of the eye arising from or occurring in more than one focus or location causing early onset macular degeneration and severely reducing one's center of vision (That's what I came to understand).]

It was a bit of an ordeal for the years to come, but we managed to get through it. We set Xander up with Braille classes in school and prepared him the best we could for a future without eyesight.

I didn't have insurance on the family at the time and Xander would require LASIK surgery once or twice a year to cauterize the ever exploding blood vessels in his eyes. It was a few thousand out of pocket each time, but it truly was money well spent.

Each time a blood vessel burst, I would sell my soul to gather the cash, and he would be zapped with the laser within days. I wish I could come up with that kinda, dough now!

My boy will be twenty this year. The blood vessels in his eyes have stopped bursting for the last few years. His vision is reduced but stable, and he was able to pass the eye exam at the DMV, which is more than I can say for myself. His only restriction on his driver's license is he must have all three mirrors in whatever vehicle he is operating.

My favorite part of all this, he drives a delivery truck for a warehouse. Dead by nine, eh? What an ass-munch. I'd like to slap the jackass doctor that said that. Remember, fifty percent of all doctors finished in the bottom half of their class. Do your own research and find one a little closer to the top.

Chapter 18:
Get a Life

You're here, that's unfortunate. This means you have bigger issues than I can fix and, quite possibly, a contributing factor as to how you got in this pickle. All that I can do is offer you some friendly advice. If this does not get you past Chapter 1, then I recommend seeking professional help immediately!

Everyone on this rock has their own reasons for wanting to be here. If you're going to succeed at this living thing, then you have to realize that there is one common thread that connects those who are really good at it. Whatever you do in this life, do it for yourself first. This has become my golden rule. Ask yourself "Does this make me feel good? Is this going to make me money? Give me pleasure? Me. Me. Me."

What's the first thing they tell you to do on a passenger plane in the event the cabin should lose pressure? Secure your own oxygen mask first before you help your neighbor.

If this sounds greedy or self-centered then good, learn to embrace these thoughts. If you're no good for yourself, then you're probably no good for anyone else. If you think these are terrible or evil thoughts, then you don't get it. Allow me to explain further.

By embracing this philosophy, correctly something dramatic will happen. Soon a smile will begin to appear on your face. People will actual want to spend time with you. You may even discover a little more cash in your pocket. Now, I'm not saying money can buy happiness, but it can sure as hell finance it. If you can be a happy person when you're broke, then you'll be ecstatic when you've got a few bucks!

Now here's the important rule. Don't be an asshole! This is a difficult balancing act when you're living this philosophy. Nobody likes an asshole. You'll notice if you're doing it wrong when your friends start dropping off the chart. Remember this: if it makes you feel good to help a friend, then do it. If you derive pleasure from giving a homeless guy a buck, then do it. If it doesn't, then don't.

There's nothing worse than asking someone to help you do something and then listen to them bitch about it the whole time. I'd rather do it by myself, regardless of the struggle.

However, it's a pleasure to do anything with someone who actually appears to be enjoying the event. Concentrating on yourself does not mean forsaking all others. If you find this rule to be difficult, then please refer to Chapter 19.

For instance, don't live for your kids, live for yourself. In this fashion, you will find yourself in a much better position to help them when they truly need you— and they will. They'll also have a much better appreciation for it when you do. Keep in mind they have to live for themselves too. If you live for them, then you have raised them to rely solely on you. If something were to happen to you, where would that leave them? They'll be fending for themselves like they should have done while you were still alive. At least then you could offer proper assistance when it is truly required. Now they're doomed.

[**doomed: to make certain the failure or destruction of**. That's right, you did this!]

See what you did?

Chapter 19:
How to Not Be an Asshole

Attitude is everything. It's important to eat a healthy plate of confidence with a slice of humble pie. There's a fine line between confident and arrogant. If you develop a "holier than thou" attitude, your friends will begin to drop like flies.

You can be the sharpest cat in the room with a pocket full of dough and a shiny new smile, but if you can't bring yourself to apologize for pissing in the front door in last night's drunken stupor, then chances are no one is going to give a shit about the fifty dollar pizza you bought everyone for dinner the night before.

A little humility goes a long, long way my friend. A long way indeed.

[**humility: The quality or state of reflecting, expressing, or offered in a spirit of deference or submission**]

Chapter 20:
Live

[**live: to have a life rich in experience**. That's what I'm talkin' 'bout.]

Live your life to the fullest. You only get one go around, so make it count. Beware of people that are overly cautious, they might turn you into a bump on a stick. Expect to make a mistake or five. Learn from them and don't repeat 'em. By the same token, don't hang with those that throw caution out the window. If you're living right, then you have caution tied securely to your leg. With enough slack to enjoy life, but not enough slack to keep you from flying out the five story window behind it when it gets tossed out first.

Always tell the truth. Don't allow yourself to get tangled up in the twisted chain of horseshit. The truth is always easier to remember than a fabrication. If people think of you as a bullshitter, then no one will take you seriously.

Always pet your woman as often as you can. If the attention connection is broken, you'll find her across the yard sniffing at a bug. Just be careful not to put all your eggs in one basket. When you need them the most, they're gone like a ghost, and you'll end up with a soggy basket of broken dreams.

Choose your battles wisely, my friends.

Remember kids, nobody's getting out of this life alive.

If all else fails, write a book!

The End

About the Cover

At the end of two thousand and nine, after I had been out of the hospital for a couple of months, I needed to make a retreat from the front. The battle was beginning to wear hard on my mental faculties, and I felt as though I was beginning to lose the war. I made a desperate phone call to my very best friend in Illinois, Paul, and pleaded for backup, "Get me the hell out of here! I need an evac, stat, or there's gonna' be carnage beyond my control." Bless his heart, I was on a plane the very next morning.

It was wintertime, and the snow was deep when I got there. Neither he, nor his wife likes to smoke in the house, although they both smoke every bit as much as I do. It was too cold outside to smoke in the porch one night, so we sat around the fireplace, drinking cocktails and blowing smoke up the chimney. We talked about everything that evening, from where I had been to where my life was going. The answers to the second half of that were eluding me, and eventually, we succumbed to the night and retired.

When Paul awoke the next morning to go to work, he saw the scene that I had left behind on the floor and snapped a shot of it on his iPhone. He texted it to me from work, and we had joked that it would have made an awesome Tom Waits album cover, and then I forgot about it.

It was a year later when I started to write this book, and I had the title right off the start. A few months later, and about half way through, it hit me like a brick; "That picture is the perfect cover!" I dug it out of my phone's memory and plastered the title on it. I emailed it to Paul, and he reconfigured the lettering, font and colors. The rest, as they say, is history...

Forge: to form or bring into being especially by an expenditure of effort.

Thank you for reading How to Survive When the Bottom Drops Out. If you have questions or comments, you may contact J.T. Sather at JTS@inknbeans.com, or like him on Facebook at http://tiny.cc/qf6isw. If you enjoyed the book, do the guy a solid and leave a review. Thank you.

Look for these other fine authors from Inknbeans Press:

Emjae Edwards, *You'll Wake Up One Morning*
Susan Wells Bennett, *The Brass Monkey Series*
Jim Burkett, *The Nick West Series*
Rusty Coats, *Out of Touch*
Kitty Sutton, *Mysteries From the Trail of Tears*
Dea Lenihan, *Out of This World Series*
Dawn Hood, *God's Pinky Promises*
David Rowinski, *The Open Pillow*
Dorothy Legge, *Poems of Faith and Love*
Ey Wade, *In My Sister's World*
Perle Butcher Lyon, *The Dutch Doctor*
Eric Pullin, *Digweed the Cat*
Hugh Ashton, *The Deed Box of John H Watson, MD*
Annarita Guarnieri. *The Importance of Being Shine*
Virginia Czaja, *Get Real*
Jackie Williams, *the Tori-Jean, No! series*
Liam McCaughey, *Collected Werks*
R.H. Ramsey. *Just Beneath the Surface II*
Robin Bee Owens: *Dabby and Maxie*

Fresh Books Brewed Daily

www.ingramcontent.com/pod-product-compliance
Lightning Source LLC
Chambersburg PA
CBHW060951040426
42445CB00011B/1109